Hampshire
Edited by Annabel Cook

First published in Great Britain in 2008 by:
Young Writers
Remus House
Coltsfoot Drive
Peterborough
PE2 9JX
Telephone: 01733 890066
Website: www.youngwriters.co.uk

All Rights Reserved

© Copyright Contributors 2008

SB ISBN 978-1 84431 627 4

Foreword

Young Writers was established in 1991 and has been passionately devoted to the promotion of reading and writing in children and young adults ever since. The quest continues today. Young Writers remains as committed to the nurturing of poetic and literary talent as ever.

This year's Young Writers competition has proven as vibrant and dynamic as ever and we are delighted to present a showcase of the best poetry from across the UK and in some cases overseas. Each poem has been selected from a wealth of *Little Laureates 2008* entries before ultimately being published in this, our seventeenth primary school poetry series.

Once again, we have been supremely impressed by the overall quality of the entries we have received. The imagination, energy and creativity which has gone into each young writer's entry made choosing the poems a challenging and often difficult but ultimately hugely rewarding task - the general high standard of the work submitted ensured this opportunity to bring their poetry to a larger appreciative audience.

We sincerely hope you are pleased with this final collection and that you will enjoy *Little Laureates 2008 Hampshire* for many years to come.

Contents

Ella Flood (9)	26
Chelsea Morris (9)	27
Luke Flanagan (9)	27
Jessica Kelly (10)	28
Nicola Goldsworthy (10)	28
Annabel Gadd (10)	29
Madison Hill (7)	29
Josie Thomas (8)	30
Natasha Scott (9)	30
Emily Paris (9)	31
Andrew Ewing (9)	31
Matthew O'Hara (9)	32
Russell Cairns (9)	32
Gemma Flint (9)	33
Eloise Oldfield (8)	33
Sam Blackwell (9)	34
Tim Lees (8)	34
Samuel Bird (9)	35
Emily Davies (8)	35
Chris Merker (11)	36
Ellen Drewe (10)	37
Will Hooper (9)	37
Peter Follett (10)	38
Alysha Taylor (9)	38
Jordan Luscombe	39
Rachel Jordan (10)	40
Eloise Joy (10)	41
Connor McCabe (11)	42
Thomas Kelly (10)	43
Max Robinson (10)	44
Damien Mony (10)	45
Annabelle Scott (10)	46
Elsie Sime (11)	47
Georgina Shipman (11)	48
Natasha Voase (8)	48
Jordan Byrne (8)	49
Lavin Deeba (9)	49
Aimee Smith (11)	50
Jonathan White (11)	51
Cori Deverick (11)	52
Morgan Attwood-Summers (10)	52
Ellen Grace O'Hara (10)	52

Lee Colegate (11)	53
Matthew Clarke (11)	53
Sophie Franklin (11)	53
Abigail Brooks (10)	54
Matthew James Williams (11)	54
Calum Rainier (8)	55
Hayley Bowen (11)	55
Jordan Scott (10)	56
Samuel James Polden (11)	56
Luke Mason (9)	57
Max Barker (8)	58
Joseph Beardsley (8)	58
Thomas Hunt (10)	59
Isabel Hensby (10)	60
Molly Ryan (9)	61
Edward Hensby (10)	62
Katriona Holroyd (9)	63
Eleanor Leiper (10)	64
Sophie Lane (9)	65
Harry Willis (9)	66
Saskia Tyler (10)	67
Charlie Jessett (9)	68
Joshua Cronin (9)	68
Ellie Morris (9)	69
Alex Keeble (9)	69
Connor West (8)	70
Beccy Mabin (9)	70
Emma Holroyd (7)	71
Sam Wright (9)	71
Rebecca Thorne (8)	72
Harry Williams (9)	72
Thomas Rowe (8)	73
James Rampton (9)	73
Kathryn Lutley (8)	74
Max Pullen (9)	74
Lorna Cook (8)	75
Rebecca Niblett (9)	75
Matthew Chapman (8)	76
Edward Moores (10)	76
Kieran Barker (11)	77
Olly Earnshaw (9)	77
Francesca Collinson (8)	78

James Grice (8)	78
Oliver Symons (8)	79
Emily Leonard (9)	79
Ellen Griffiths (8)	80
Megan Mulcahy (8)	80
Leander Rodricks (9)	81
Jessica Bell-Noad (8)	81
Phoebe Busbridge (10)	82
Jessica Gollop (11)	83
James Boyle & David Cook (10)	84
Abigail Mikowski (8)	84
Zoe Bradley (10)	85
Sarah Thornton (8)	86
Emily Robinson (11)	86
Daisy Hales (8)	87
Elena Mesri (8)	87
Joshua Wright (8)	88
Sam Amiri (8)	88

Ashford Hill Primary School

Kelly-May Black (10)	88
Athina Giles (9)	88
Katie Victoria Lobo (10)	89
Daniella Butler (8)	89
Bethany Leah Rain (9)	90
Kayleigh Claire Wickenden (8)	90
Gregory Adam (10)	91
Heather Smyth (9)	91
Molly Lawrence (8)	92
Brandon Collins (9)	92
Callum Hall (10)	93
Samuel Maya (9)	93
Holly Olivia Hathaway (8)	94
Rebecca Quelch (9)	94
Georgia Martin-Smythe (9)	95

Craneswater Junior School

Elliott Robinson (10)	95
Jessica Wall (11)	96
Louise Gordon (9)	96
Freya Noble (10)	97

Millie Garside (9)	97
Jessica Palmer (10)	98
Kirsty Broadway (9)	98
Amy Johnson (9)	99
Isobel Terry (8)	99
Emily Nagel (11)	100
Eoghan D'All (11)	101
Noah Clements (10)	102
Joshua Gillmore (9)	103
Jessica Nickerson (11)	103
Molly Hipkin (10)	104
Beth Linford (7)	104
Marina Sealey (11)	105
George Green (8)	106
Sophie Nickerson (10)	106
Fatima Khatun (9)	107
Gurdit Singh Digpal (10)	108
Monica Boulton (10)	108
Karamjot Kaur (10)	109
Alice Kellam (10)	110
Terrianne Carter (9)	110
Amina Souhaid (9)	111
Josh Tuck (9)	111
Gloria Truscott (10)	112
Sofaya Looker-Ere (7)	113
Ruby Lepora (7)	114
Millie Lepora (9)	114
Jordan Grattan (7)	114
Joseph Laithwaite (11)	115
Samantha Mapulango Dimingo (8)	115
Megan Linford (10)	116
Jamshed Gafarov (9)	116
Hanley Morgan (8)	117
Miki Ginns (8)	117
Nicole Poore (11)	118
Jacob Thomas (7)	118

Gomer Junior School

Emily Hall (11)	119
Alex Clements (11)	119
Katie Walters (11)	120

Elizabeth Steer (11)	120
Lauren Mose (10)	120
Natasha Barker (11)	121
Genevieve Norris (11)	121
Katie Bird (10)	122
Hayley Westmorland (10)	122
Connor Powell (11)	123
Ellen Watts (11)	123
Joe Bavister (10)	124
Natalie Neal (11)	124
Nathan Sitch (10)	125
Elin Bebbington (10)	125
Olivia Webb (11)	126
Jonathan Eaton (11)	126
Alice Cowan (10)	126
Rowan Pierce (11)	127
Emma Newman (10)	127
Sommer Rawlinson (11)	128

Heatherside Junior School
Emma Higham (10)	128
Alice Pooley (10)	129
Padraíg Manning (9)	130
Emmie Mynott (10)	131
Alice Proctor (9)	132
Emily Barden (9)	133
Zoe Styles (10)	134
Amy Miller (10)	135
Georgia Haldenby (9)	136
Isabelle Davies (9)	137
Kemba Mitchell (10)	138
Eve Boulter (10)	139
Hayley Johnston (10)	140

John Keble CE Primary School
Anastasia Pybus (8)	140
Eryn Tyler-Smith (9)	141
Georgia Lacey (8)	141
Oliver Piper (8)	142
Jason Symons (8)	142
Jonathan Greene (8)	143

Amelia Victoria (8)	143
Amy Joseph (9)	144
Calvin Jarman (8)	144
Ellie Dickson (8)	145
George Rayner (8)	145
Cameron Thomson (7)	146
Ethan Pell (8)	146
Katie Williamson-Jones (8)	146
Rosie Welch (7)	147
Emma Harwood (9)	147
Jonathan Ling (8)	147
Mason Tyler-Smith (7)	148
Frankie Taylor (9)	148
Emily Baker (8)	149
Lula Dickson (7)	149
Joe Arthur (8)	150
Jehian Tiley (7)	150
Lalie Carlod (9)	150
Bea Golley (8)	151
Charles Hurst (7)	151
Ellie Mackinnon (9)	151

Knights Enham Junior School

Shannon Allen (10)	152
Chelsee James (10)	152
Deanne Johnson-May (10)	152
Maya Loaiza (9)	153
Sky Charmaine Taylor (9)	153
Abi Buckland (9)	153
Keeya Hanley (9)	154
Deanna Archer (10)	154
Matthew Blake (9)	154
Connor Durbridge (9)	155
Jade Goddard (9)	155
Abbie Jessica Haswell (10)	155
Kurtis Archer (11)	156
Bruce Shaw (10)	156
Billy Duffy (11)	157
Tom Lant (9)	157
Kirsten Armstrong (10)	158
Kaitlin Fairchild (10)	158

Laura Hanson (9)	158
Callum Paxton (10)	159
Gemma Blake (9)	159
Chloe Gleed (9)	159
Katie Dutton (10)	160
Jessica Hall (9)	160
Brendan Harris (10)	161
Matthew Lovering (10)	161
Jack Tough (10)	162
Frankie Horton (9)	162
Nicole Underhill (9)	162
Katie Turner (10)	163
Jade Trowbridge (9)	163
Charlie Sweet (11)	164
Dominic Howitt (11)	164
Carma Newell (10)	165
Shannon Maxim (10)	165

Milton Park Junior School
Ben Ireland (11)	166
Brandon Shaw (10)	166
Alexander Whitcomb (10)	166

Oakfield Primary School
Adrienne Godden (10)	167
Dee-Cha Henderson (9)	167
Laura Brooks (10)	168

St Winifred's School, Southampton
Lars Meidell (8)	168
George Parrott (8)	169
Georgia Parker (11)	169
Adam Johnston (11)	170
Emily Lewis (11)	170
Samuel Riley (9)	171
Sanjiv Gill (8)	171
Jeevan Sahota (7)	172
Stephen Whorwood (10)	172
Tristan Harley (11)	172
Joseph Seymour (10)	173
George Vincent (8)	173

Simon Solecki (8)	173
Alice Borodzicz (10)	174
Kieran Harrison (7)	174
Victor Smith (8)	175
Alice Denham (10)	175
Samuel Johnson	175
Francesca Mylod-Ford (9)	176
Stephen Follows (9)	176
Max McHugh (9)	177
Orla McGinnis (8)	177

Steep CE Primary School

Flora Burleigh (11)	177
Joshua Rolison (10)	178
Amy Jo Holden (9)	178
Dominic Young-Ballinger (9)	178
Reuben Harry (9)	179
Cameron Martin (11)	179
Evelyn Kay Blackwell (9)	179
Jack Evans (11)	180
John Mackey (10)	180
Stephen Miller (11)	180
Ella Williamson (11)	181
Katriona Pritchard (9)	181
Ellie Hitchcock (9)	181
Sophie Topps (10)	182

Tower Hill Primary School

Megan Tompkins (8)	182
Daniel Beers-Baker (10)	183
Klara Cheetham (9)	183
Jordan Greentree (9)	183
Alexandra Groves (9)	184
Megan Stimson (8)	184
George Griffiths (9)	184
Matthew Spencer (9)	185
George Sidney (10)	185
Callum Gribble (10)	186
Charlie Pearson (11)	186
Zak De Bruyn (7)	186
Chloe Skinner (11)	187

Connor Griffiths (11)	187
Jordan Sayers (8)	187
Bradley (11)	188
Rai Hemant Kumar (11)	188
James Cook (7)	188
Nadine Drew (11)	189
Courtney Bell (11)	189
Nikki Pauline Hayes (8)	189
Kerry Peace (10)	190
Johnny Whitehead (10)	190
Daniel Freke (11)	190
Kitty Roberts (11)	191
Michael Crowhurst (10)	191
Kallum Chivers (10)	191
Jordan Powell (10)	192
Lewis Anderton (11)	192
Tom Spencer (10)	193
Selvy Yasotharan (11)	193

The Poems

The Alien Has Landed

It was a windy twilight,
So cold and foggy,
Faint sounds of an owl hooting,
The gravestones black and scary.

The earth began to shake,
Dirt and grass flew everywhere,
Then a great, enormous hole appeared,
Full of a blinding light.

A spaceship stopped suddenly with a screech
And a massive door opened,
Then a pair of glowing eyes,
Belonging to an alien coming out.

The alien looked like a rainbow
With eyes like a torch.
He didn't look scary,
But how would we know?

Amy Holifield (10)
All Saints CE Junior School

Time

Tick-tock, tick-tock,
Time to tell a clock,
The clock shows time.

Tick-tock, tick-tock,
Time to look at the past.
The past was hours before.

Tick-tock, tick-tock,
Welcome to the wonder of history,
Of history many years ago.

Tick-tock, tick-tock,
Time is always here.

Daniel Tu (9)
All Saints CE Junior School

The Aliens Have Landed

It was cold and boggy in the field.
The lights were all blacked out.
Nothing interesting ever happened,
Life was boring, without a doubt.

Whirling leaves were flying about,
A scary whirlwind sound,
Nature was flying everywhere,
Including worms from the ground.

A ramp appeared from the UFO,
Quietly sliding down
Then it walked along the steps,
Creeping around our town.

Its eyes were like the golden sun
Gleaming down at me,
Its spindly legs were stumbling around,
Its chest was as solid as a tree.

Rachel Warwick (10)
All Saints CE Junior School

Blackberrying

Here comes autumn.
I see a messy mayhem of twists and turns.
Here comes autumn.
I hear birds singing and trees rustling.
Here comes autumn.
I smell the air, fresh and clean.
Here comes autumn.
I feel the squishy, soft blackberries and spiky thorns.
Here comes autumn.
I taste the sweet jammy taste of blackberries.
Here comes autumn.

James Wheeler (8)
All Saints CE Junior School

The Aliens Have Landed

It was raining heavily in the field,
Animals tiptoeing,
Ready to be killed.
Minibeasts scuttling,
Silent as could be.
Everything silent, everything still
As I could see.

A wind was blowing in the air,
Earth breaking,
Finding a lair,
Shivering skin,
Wishing I had care,
Something landed, tall and wide,
Looking like a bear.

In a forest, as chilly as could be,
Creatures searching,
Looking for me.
A short shadow
As quiet as could be,
An alien so smooth and so strong
Staring at me.

So wide and so tall,
Legs were thin,
As round as a rugby ball.
Walking quietly,
Three eyes ready to call,
Body ready to fall.

Vincent Tu (10)
All Saints CE Junior School

The Aliens Have Landed

It was a clear cold night when the sky was dark,
Frost was thick on the ground and coating trees' bark,
Snow started coming, light at first,
Then it came down in a sudden great burst.
It was forever the same.

A terrible rumble broke into the peace,
A squawk and then gone were the geese.
A circle appeared as the frost melted,
The noise got louder till out it belted.
It was almost always the same.

Then all of a sudden, out of thin air,
Appeared a creature from his bright lair.
He was silhouetted against the light behind,
No one could see his face but he didn't seem kind.
It just wasn't the same.

Out came a robot searching for life,
It found a rabbit and then with a knife,
He poked it aboard the invisible ship
And the door closed with a big blip.
It was no longer the same.

Then just when this poem was going to end,
Straight ahead and round the bend,
The blobby alien appeared with the poor rabbit,
He set it free to go back to its old habit.
It was never the same.

Grace Howard (11)
All Saints CE Junior School

The Senses Whisper

(Based on 'The Sound Collector' by Roger McGough)

An odd thing happened to me today,
A whisper whooshed right past me,
He took every single sense
And left me aghast.

The smell of fresh cut grass
On a beautiful warm spring morn,
The look of happiness
As my favourite boots are worn.

The touch of a baby's skin,
Perfect, cute and sweet,
The small hands, button nose
And faultless titchy feet.

The sight of my dog's smiling face
As I run to him and laugh,
Brushing past the bright flowers
Lining his garden path.

The sound of the soft music,
Melodies rise and fall,
Will I one day be part of that
In that magnificent concert hall?

The taste of Mum's pancakes,
My sister's eaten four!
But however many she can eat,
I can eat more!

Jamie Cunningham (11)
All Saints CE Junior School

Ice

Ice starts as water,
Then at zero degrees
The water turns to ice
As solid as a rock.
Yet slippery as a long stripy snake.
Ice is as smooth as a young child's face,
Perfect for people to ride,
Whizzing around on snow-white blades,
Or to gracefully push and glide,
Some slipping over,
Landing on the rock-like pool
And bumping as they fall.
All through the winter,
Ice stays rigid
Like a see-through,
Square,
Churned-up grid . . .

Sophie Gould (11)
All Saints CE Junior School

Leopards

Leopards are great animals,
Queens of the jungle.
They're as fierce as fire,
Yet firm as a brick.

Leopards are spotty animals,
They blend and stay still,
Waiting to catch their prey.

Leopards are great animals,
Queens of the jungle,
They're as fierce as fire,
Yet as firm as a brick.

Olivia Mist (10)
All Saints CE Junior School

Snow

As the snow falls over the trees
It looks like vanilla ice cream.
I can feel the soft, crumbly snow
Falling through my fingertips.
I can smell the waft of the kitchen,
Pouring out the smell like a tap.

People are flying over jumps like Evel Knievel,
You can hear technically sound skiers
Carving out turns.

Up in the chairlifts you can see
Children laughing as a friend
Tells them the best joke ever.
Young children shrieking
Like newborn chicks.

Ross McMichael (11)
All Saints CE Junior School

Cheetahs

The fastest animal on the track,
Ready, steady, go.
The wind it races, it's gathering its paces,
Ready, steady, go.
A golden-brown, like an autumn leaf,
Ready, steady, go.
The sand the colour of the rising sun,
Ready, steady, go.
As fast and courageous as a lion or snake,
Ready, steady, go.
But soon it is out of breath, alas,
Ready, steady, stop.

Benjamin Robert Hood (11)
All Saints CE Junior School

Water

I started in the ocean in the crashing foamy waves,
I've flowed in raging rivers, huge mountains, cliffs and caves.
You've seen me in the boiling summer, soaking fields of corn,
And wiped me from your windowpane upon a frosty morn.

I've fallen with the snowflakes, keeping school kids home from class,
They've rolled me in their snowmen and I've heard
their screams and laughs.
You've spied me splashing colours in a rainbow way up high
And watched me join with others making cloud shapes in the sky.

Melissa Holt (10)
All Saints CE Junior School

The Rain

The rain is falling like tip-tapping shoes,
Little blue puddles shining in the sun.
When it pours down it's like someone's emptied
a bucket full of water,
Hailstones falling like someone sieving bits of stones
out of a pile of mud,
When there's thunder the rain is angry,
But still the rain is so cool.

Jake Hammond (11)
All Saints CE Junior School

Snow

As the torrential snow started pouring down, down and down,
It started to dance like a whipping volcano,
It started twirling round, round and round.
When you touched it, it was so cool,
Like a cold, dark swimming pool.
It came down as fast as lightning,
Like little people fighting!

Chloe Moreton (10)
All Saints CE Junior School

The Senses Gone

(Based on 'The Sound Collector' by Roger McGough)

An unusually weird thing happened,
A cold air rushed right past,
It flew with incredible speed
And left my room last.

It collected all the senses,
The smell of flowers
And home-made cakes,
Then left the cowards.

It collected all the senses,
The taste of apple pie,
The look of disappointment,
The happiness now a lie.

A touch of fur on a dog's back,
Perfect, soft and smooth,
The touch of bark on a crumbled tree,
The leaves gently move.

The sight of my friend's smile
Makes me laugh with joy,
Rushing past all the plants,
Gaining a lovely toy.

The sound of the crowd singing
As I score a perfect goal,
Will I score again
And complete my goal?

All the things disappeared,
But wait! Look at the big red sack,
The cold air has returned
And brought the senses back.

Matthew Chiverton (10)
All Saints CE Junior School

A Poem For All Seasons

Easter eggs at Easter time,
The people ready to play football, to have fun,
Rabbits jumping around the wood as carefree as children,
The flowers coming up in the frosty grass,
Days getting longer and more time to play,
The Premiership champions jumping around in joy.

People excited about their holidays,
People having birthdays,
People having a barbecue,
Running to the clear crystal sea,
Shouting in the swimming pool,
Fresh start of the Premiership.

The leaves turning brown,
Leaves crackling on the floor,
Hallowe'en letting people scare others,
People jumping into leaf piles,
Fireworks and bonfires crackling,
A time of change from greens to orange.

Making snowmen,
Having a snowball fight,
People opening presents,
Christmas is coming to town,
Wrapping up warm in scarves and gloves,
Then New Year's Eve for the new start.

Luke Brown (10)
All Saints CE Junior School

A Poem For All Seasons

The bursting blossom coming to life,
The colours of a butterfly's wings fluttering,
Baby chicks hatching out of their eggs,
Bright green leaves waiting to come out,
Greens, purples, oranges and yellows all over the place,
Children playing on the grass.

Roses as red as a burning fire,
Water splashing and shouts of laughter,
Sunglasses, T-shirts, shorts coming out,
The blue, clear sky, not a cloud in sight.
The cool, small breeze brushing against you,
The heat of the yellow summer sun.

The crunch of the leaves underneath people's feet,
The fading of people's gardens from summer,
The leaves twirling and twisting as they fall to the ground,
Bonfires and fireworks popping in the cold sky,
Hallowe'en sweets and candy.

Winter is full of cold and rain,
The snow as white as clouds,
Snow on Christmas Day,
Children in scarves and warm clothes,
Fires glowing brightly at Christmas,
Laughter of children building snowmen.

Rosanna Ashford (9)
All Saints CE Junior School

A Poem For All Seasons

Leaves and blossom on the dull, dark trees,
Flowers pop out of the dark squelchy mud,
Eggs hatch and chicks poke their heads out of their cream shells,
Rivers flowing and families eating picnics,
Baby lambs jumping around the bright green grass,
Birds catching food for lunch.

The sun gets hotter than fire,
The sand boils your feet,
Children swimming in the turquoise water,
Music playing for children's birthdays,
People doing races on sports day,
People packing for summer holidays.

People dressed as witches and ghosts collecting lots of sweets,
Crackling bonfires and sparkling fireworks,
The temperature drops and leaves fall from the trees,
People buying pumpkins and carving scary faces,
Pumpkins glowing in windows,
Skeletons on people's doors.

People put up Christmas trees,
And footprints in the snow,
People singing Christmas carols,
People making giant snowmen with pointed carrot noses,
Children shouting on Christmas Day
And putting out carrots for Rudolph.

Eloise Clarke (9)
All Saints CE Junior School

A Poem For All Seasons

The green grass growing rapidly in the fields,
The birth of new animals in spring,
Leaves growing back on trees,
Animals waking from hibernation to see the lovely colours of spring,
Lambs jumping around as happy as can be,
Days getting longer for more time to play.

The sun getting hotter, beating on the earth,
People having picnics on beautiful green grass fields,
Football being played as people are getting hot and sweaty,
People are playing at the beach while the sand is still very hot,
Summer is a time when we have our holidays,
A time of fun and laughter.

Bonfires start as people start burning things,
Leaves fall off trees and start to turn brown,
Conker fights start, which turn into fights,
People getting costumes for spooky Hallowe'en,
Hedgehogs finding places to hibernate for winter,
Leaves getting crunched underfoot.

People getting excited as Christmas is near,
People getting wrapped up as the days get colder,
Snowball fights start, which turn into riots,
Footprints being made in the white snow,
Frost on windows while people are sitting in their homes,
A time of comfort in houses.

James Evans (10)
All Saints CE Junior School

Number Poem

I've got a new best mate . . .
His name is Seven.

We met on the seventh day of Christmas,
He bought me seven presents.

I played with him all last week.
On the first day we played footy and drew 7-7.

On the second day we bought a lottery ticket.
We were supposed to choose six numbers, but I chose seven.
I had to choose the number 49, it's 7 x 7.

On the third day we did my tables together,
And it was the 7x tables.

On the fourth day we played on the Wii,
Altogether we played seven games.

On the fifth day we played charades
And Seven was acting odd.

On the sixth day it was my brother's birthday.
He was greedy and had seven slices of birthday cake.

On the last day we were quite fat from the cake
So we went to the gym.
I lost seven pounds and Seven wasn't in bad shape either.
(In fact he was a heptagon, so he was like a 50p.)

That's why I love the number seven.

Oliver Hughes (10)
All Saints CE Junior School

A Poem For All Seasons

Spring brings flowers, taking over the dullness,
The empty blue sky swells with light,
The air, crisp and fresh on a cold spring morning,
Easter eggs hidden in the lush green grass,
Lambs are born, bounding and jumping,
Spring is bright and reflective.

Summer brings holidaying on tropical islands,
Licking ice lollies like a frog catching flies,
Hiking hills in the summer heat,
Family picnics under the burning sun,
Out of school, no more classes,
Summer is a time of relaxation.

Autumn brings animals hibernating under bushes,
Planting pumpkins with Grandad and Father,
Leaves turn brown, yellow and purple,
Autumn sky as dull as an empty room,
Diving into leaf piles to pass your time away,
Autumn is a time of fun and enjoyment.

Winter brings snow and snowman fun,
Birds using feeders and houses,
Christmas joy brings anticipation,
Jumping in frozen puddles,
Winter sky as cold as ice,
Winter is a time of wrapping up warm.

Katie Fowles (10)
All Saints CE Junior School

The Whisper Of The Senses

(Based on 'The Sound Collector' by Roger McGough)

A strange thing occurred today,
A whisper whooshed right past,
Gathered every single sense,
Super quick then fast.

The smell of fresh warm bread,
Straight out of the baker's,
The look of disappointment
When I run out of capers.

The touch of a baby's skin,
Perfect, soft and sweet,
The dimpled hands, button nose
And faultless tiny feet.

The sight of my gran's smiling face
As I run to her and laugh,
Brushing past the vivid flowers
Lining her garden path.

The sound of beautiful music,
Melodies rise and fall,
Will you one day be a part of that
In that magnificent concert hall?

The taste of my mum's pancakes,
My brother's eaten four!
But however many he can eat,
I can manage more!

All these things have disappeared,
But wait! Look back along the track.
The whisper has returned once more
And brought the senses back!

Javin Fletcher (10)
All Saints CE Junior School

The Senses Stealer

(Based on 'The Sound Collector' by Roger McGough)

A strange thing happened to us today,
An odd thing whooshed right past,
Banished every wonderful sense
And left us all aghast.

The smell of fresh cut grass
On a beautiful new spring day,
The look of disappointment
On a cold wet day of May.

The sound of my brother's loud music,
A blast that's loud and clear,
The scream of my cute second cousins,
A sound that I often hear.

The sight of my mum's favourite dress
In the bright and shimmering light,
Looking at my brand new book,
The cover's nice and bright.

The happiness that comes
When they compliment my voice,
I want to choose a melody,
But they say it's not my choice.

The taste of my favourite roast dinner,
Potatoes, chicken and all,
My favourite chocolate cake's up next,
It's round, plump and tall.

The senses vanished one by one,
That strange thing stole them all,
But look, it's coming back right now,
It's placed the senses in the hall!

Laura Edis (10)
All Saints CE Junior School

The Feeling

(Based on 'The Sound Collector' by Roger McGough)

A weird thing happened to me today,
A whisper jumped right past,
Collected every known sense
And left us all aghast.

The smell of freshly-made bread
No a lovely warm spring morn,
The disappointed look,

The soft touch of a baby's skin,
Complete, pretty, smooth,
The dimpled hands, button nose
And sweet tiny feet move to the groove.

The sight of my dog's face
As I run to him and play,
Sprinting past my dad
In the massive field today.

The sound of the TV,
The dog's getting a groom,
Will I one day be part of it
In my front room?

The taste of my brother's cheesecake,
My dad's eaten half,
He is guzzling them down by the second,
He has spilt some on my scarf.

All these are gone.
Oh yes, they're back,
He has returned once more
And it wasn't black.

Nathan Chaplin (10)
All Saints CE Junior School

The Senses Snatcher

(Based on 'The Sound Collector' by Roger McGough)

A weird thing happened to us today,
A snatcher zoomed right past,
Gathered every single sense
And left us all aghast.

The smell of the cooking burger
On a greasy, warm, green grill,
The look of disappointment
As my favourite burger began to frill.

The touch of ketchup,
Perfect, delicious and sweet,
As it squirts on the hot burger,
I squirt it to a funky beat.

The look on my dad's angry face,
I accidentally squirted it on his best trousers,
Brushing past the back door
Getting ready to beat the bowsers.

The sound of the crackling burger,
The smoke rises and falls,
Will I one day be able to eat my burger
In those magnificent eating halls?

The taste of my mum's burping cake,
My brother's burped the most!
But even though I can't win,
He doesn't have to boast!

All these things have vanished,
But wait! The look on his face.
The snatcher has returned once more
And put the senses in the wrong place.

James Miles (11)
All Saints CE Junior School

The Weird Feeling

(Based on 'The Sound Collector' by Roger McGough)

A strange thing happened to me today,
A weird feeling galloped past,
Collecting all the odd touches
And left me running fast.

The spongy touch of the cake,
My mother's beautiful cooking,
It is taken away, being stolen,
On his back, hooking.

The weird thought of my violin bow
Being carried away,
Rotting as time goes by,
Or using it as a fishing rod.

The smooth touch of the fireplace
As he collects the flower pots,
It is a horrible thought,
The warmth taken away.

The squeaky noise
Of the ponies crying out,
I feel so sorry for them
As they are loaded onto a truck.

Hannah Caulfield (10)
All Saints CE Junior School

Time

Tick-tock, tick-tock,
Time to go to bed,
To bed you go.

Tick-tock, tick-tock,
Time to tell a story of adventure,
Of adventure I will say today.

Tick-tock, tick-tock,
Time is flying by.

Georgina Thompson (8)
All Saints CE Junior School

The Aliens Have Landed

It was raining heavily in the field,
So chilly and so bleak,
Animals preyed amongst the trees,
It was always the same.

A humming sensation fractured the peace,
Hot air swirled around,
A silver disc floated above,
This was not the same.

The metal hatch swung open low,
He trod out purposefully,
His feet were placed with intricate care,
It would never happen again.

His feet were webbed and giant,
His whole body red,
His legs were long and bony,
He was not the same.

Georgia Smith (11)
All Saints CE Junior School

Time

Tick-tock, tick,
A mouse runs out of his hole,
A farmer's cat comes padding in
And smells him out for dinner.

Tick-tock, tick,
A horse runs in her field.
A calf is there too,
Drinking milk from her mother.

Tick-tock, tick,
A fox is lurking round a corner,
Spying on a crowd of chickens.

Laima Sinka (8)
All Saints CE Junior School

The Aliens Have Landed

It was calm before they arrived,
The moon was bright in the starry sky,
The grass that carpeted the ground was damp,
Then a phosphorescence came like a lamp!

An engine whirred,
The grass started dancing,
The ground began to shake,
But it wasn't an earthquake.

A spaceship had surfaced
And a hatch slowly opened.
An alien came out,
It had three arms, no doubt!

Its green-masked head
Supported some horns,
Its black slit eyes
Were anything but warm!

Suddenly it came,
The dawn shining through,
The thing backed away,
Leaving behind the grass and mildew.

Alice Peplow (10)
All Saints CE Junior School

Time

Tick-tock, tick-tock,
Time to see the past,
The past full of mystery.

Tick-tock, tick-tock,
Time for the present,
The present is now.

Tick-tock, tick-tock,
Time to look at the future,
The future will be fantastic.

Austin Warwick (9)
All Saints CE Junior School

The Aliens Have Landed

It was a night like any other,
Darkness muffling the air,
The sleeping village was peaceful,
Oblivious to the events looming.

A sequence of uninvited tremors
Engulfed the farmer's field,
Spurts of soil were thrown out of the ground
And a shiny spaceship appeared.

A hiss echoed eerily as the hatch opened,
The grinding engine stopped,
Out of the ship stepped a green figure,
A ghostly alien had emerged.

It had fingers as long as seaweed
And flippers for feet,
Two purple horns poked out of its head,
A warning to those it meets.

Clare Braganza (11)
All Saints CE Junior School

Time

Tick-tock, tick-tock,
Time to dress up,
Dress up as a Victorian.

Tick-tock, tick-tock,
Time to see into the future,
The future full of mystery and history.

Tick-tock, tick-tock,
Time to jump back to the Tudor time,
Tudor time was 1484 to 1602.

Tick-tock, tick-tock,
Time to research on the computer about the past,
The past where it was a thousand years ago,
Or just a minute ago.

Alex Ivey (9)
All Saints CE Junior School

The Aliens Have Landed

It was raining heavily in the field,
So damp and so bleak,
Villagers saw no excitement around,
It was always the same.

Then it arrived without a sound,
The ground below shook around,
The leaves spun a rhythmic twirl.
It couldn't ever be the same.

The air hissed as the hatch flew open,
A tentacle emerged, a camera atop,
To check to see if anyone was around.
Could it ever be the same?

Its chest as gold as the sun,
Lanky legs and arms squirming around,
Blood-red eyes, razor ears on top of a football-shaped head,
It would never be the same.

Benny Clark (10)
All Saints CE Junior School

Friendship

F riends are like flowers
R ainbow has a colour for everyone
I ce and snow are like friends
E ndings, will never end with friends
N eat circles will make better friends
D iamonds all over the place, that means friends
S hadows appear and that means friends
H igh towers of people who are friends
I gloos are places to meet better friends
P eople enjoy having friends.

Emily Lambourne (7)
All Saints CE Junior School

The Aliens Have Landed!

The pond at twilight was quiet, except for the birds cheeping away,
The other mammals resting asleep,
The water calm in the open creek,
Then the silence broke all around.

A noise louder but the same noise of a car revving,
The sound could be heard from afar,
It hid the sound of the drunks in a bar,
The alien emerged from the ship.

He came with light and noise,
No wonder no one saw him because he was the size of a pencil,
His baby would be the size of a writing utensil.
He jumped in the air to get attention.

He was as smart as Albert Einstein,
His hands were as small as a baby's,
No wonder he was a hit with the ladies.
His head was like a balloon!

Jonny McIlroy (10)
All Saints CE Junior School

My Cat Henry

M ysterious cats hunt for food
Y elling mice scamper away

C areless dogs chase their lunch
A mazingly you can hear them going *munch, munch, munch*
T rees sway with happiness while they stop the chase

H orses neigh and roll around in mud
E ager to have lots of fun all day
N ests stay on tall treetops
R ats roam round in the bright sun
Y elping birds sing with glory.

Katie Errington (10)
All Saints CE Junior School

Number Poem

I have a confession . . .
I'm in love with the number five.

Ever since I started school at five,
I've loved the number five.

It was the fifth number I could count to
And the second times table I learnt.

As soon as I was ten,
I learnt five was a prime number and it was a factor of ten.

I went to the school disco, but I was only allowed
Five cups of lemonade and five bags of crisps.

There were five songs
Before the fire bell rang for five minutes flat!

And that's why I love the number five!

Sophie Voase (10)
All Saints CE Junior School

Sue And The Rocket

There once was a wire-worked rocket,
But out came the powerful socket,
The rocket fell down,
Straight into the town,
And the townspeople started to mock it.

There once was a lady called Sue,
Who couldn't fit into her shoe,
Her shoes are size fifty,
(No wonder she's shifty!)
They're sometimes used as a canoe!

Ella Flood (9)
All Saints CE Junior School

Number Poems

I have a confession, I have a best friend, his name is Three,
I've known him longer than I've known myself.

Three days ago I went to the fair, the rides cost £3.
I went on all three rides. $3 \times 3 = 9$.
I was amazed there were only three people there.

I got a free sweet for going on the bouncy castle three times.
It was great, everything $= 3$.
I love Three so I'm always going to keep him.

On my birthday I was amazed at
What was on my cake, it was number 3.

It is - 3 degrees today. $3 \times 1 = 3$.
There are three people in my family.

I went to a restaurant today,
I had three meals to choose from.
Three is my best friend.

Chelsea Morris (9)
All Saints CE Junior School

Cathedrals - Guildford

G lorious Guildford, glamorous red brick
U nbelievable beauty, universe of God
I llustrious design, incredible golden angel
L ong nave, lined with glory
D elightful Jesus, debut of God
F resh opening of baptism, fond of the Lord
O pen spaces of praising
R anks of the Holy Order
D rink holy wine, dedicate your life.

Luke Flanagan (9)
All Saints CE Junior School

Number Poem

You know, I have a lucky number,
Most people do. Mine is the number 10!

$5 \times 2 = 10$
$10 \times 1 = 10$
Lots of things equal 10 actually,
But I was ecstatic when it came up on my birthday cake.

We went to the bingo once and
The last number we needed was 10
And we won, we won £10 grand.

I was 10 when we went to the BBC.
I spent £10 on the best thing ever.
You might not think it is but to me it is,
It's a stone carved number 10!
It touched my heart when I saw it.

Did you know $50 \div 5 = 10$?
That's why it's my lucky number.

Jessica Kelly (10)
All Saints CE Junior School

Night

M agical moonlight memorised
O cean sways over the horizon
O pen its shine to all far down
N ames itself the twirling fairy
L ands its light on your skin
I only see the moon above in the twinkling sky
G limmers as the eye can see
H igh, so high, so high
T hanking the moon for all its shine.

Nicola Goldsworthy (10)
All Saints CE Junior School

Number Poem

My mate, number 25,
Is really cool!
We are so close.

We were friends from the beginning,
Me and 25.
Without 25, we'd be in a lot of trouble.

25 is a quarter of 100, you know.
$100 \times 100 = 1,000$.
$1,000 \times 1,000 =$ one million.
A million x a million $=$ a squillion.

I am looking out of my window,
Counting the robins in the garden.
There are $5 + 5 + 5 + 5 + 5 = 25$,
Or for short, $5 \times 5 = 25$.
5×5 is a square number too!

But I know one thing,
Whatever happens,
I'll never part with 25!

Annabel Gadd (10)
All Saints CE Junior School

Friends

F antastic times
R emember who your real friends are
I n bad times they get you through
E ach day be a friend
N o one knows you like your friends
D on't pull apart any friends
S omething is there to connect you.

Madison Hill (7)
All Saints CE Junior School

Time

Tick-tock, tick-tock,
Time to tell a story,
A story of the season.

Tick-tock, tick-tock,
Time to enter spring.
Spring bursts into life and wonder.

Tick-tock, tick-tock,
Time to visit summer.
The summer is hot and relaxing.

Tick-tock, tick-tock,
Time to visit autumn.
The leaves fall in autumn.

Tick-tock, tick-tock,
Time to visit winter.
Cold and chilly, icy and windy.

Josie Thomas (8)
All Saints CE Junior School

The Clock

Tick-tock, tick-tick,
Goes the big clock.
Tick-tock, tick-tock,
Will it ever stop?

History is being made
Every hour of the day,
Tick-tock,
Ding, dong.

Tick-tock, tick-tock,
Tick-tock, tick-tock,
Tickety-tock,
Tickety-tock.

Time is always there.

Natasha Scott (9)
All Saints CE Junior School

Tick-Tock

Tick-tock, tick-tock,
Time to tell a story
About the four seasons.

Tick-tock, tick-tock,
Time to get out the pool,
Summer's here, the sun is shining.

Tick-tock, tick-tock,
Time to watch the leaves
Fall off the trees.

Tick-tock, tick-tock,
Time to wrap up warm,
Winter's on its way.

Tick-tock, tick-tock,
Time to see the beautiful blossom,
Springtime is fresh and bright.

Emily Paris (9)
All Saints CE Junior School

Time

Tick-tock, tick-tock,
Time to read a story,
A story of world war.

Tick-tock, tick-tock,
Time to enter the battlefield,
A battlefield full of dead grass.

Tick-tock, tick-tock,
Time to hide in the shelter,
A shelter made from blunt metal.

Tick-tock, tick-tock,
Time to go back home,
A home full of loving family.

Tick-tock.

Andrew Ewing (9)
All Saints CE Junior School

Tick-Tock

Tick-tock, tick-tock,
Time to tell a story,
A story of the four seasons.

Tick-tock, tick-tock,
Time to wrap up warm for the winter.
Winter, a time of freezes and frosts.

Tick-tock, tick-tock,
Time to prepare for autumn.
Autumn, a time of red and brown leaves.

Tick-tock, tick-tock,
Time to get ready for summer.
Summer, time to go to the beach.

Tick-tock, tick-tock,
Time for warm spring,
A time of picnics and fun.

Matthew O'Hara (9)
All Saints CE Junior School

Time

Tick-tock, tick-tock,
It's snowing all around,
All around it's wintertime.

Tick-tock, tick-tock,
All the new birds cheeping,
Birds cheeping in the spring morning.

Tick-tock, tick-tock,
The summer sun is burning,
Sun is burning over the dried ground.

Tick-tock, tick-tock,
All the leaves falling,
Leaves fall throughout the autumn days.

Tick-tock, tick-tock.

Russell Cairns (9)
All Saints CE Junior School

The History Clock

Tick-tock, tick-tock,
Time to learn some history,
Some history about a world war.

Tick-tock, tick-tock,
Time to enter the battlefield,
The battlefield filled with terror.

Tick-tock, tick-tock,
Time to hide in the shelter,
The shelter filled with scared soldiers.

Tick-tock, tick-tock,
Time to go back home,
Back home to an anxious family.

Tick-tock, tick-tock.

Gemma Flint (9)
All Saints CE Junior School

Blackberrying

Autumn is coming,
I see red, green and black berries
Waiting to be picked.
Autumn is coming,
I hear whistling wind
Rustling the leaves
On the blackberry shrub.
Autumn is coming,
I feel the spiky, ferocious thorns
Piecing my skin as
I reach out to pick a fruit.
Autumn is coming,
I taste the bitter blackberries
As I bite into the sour flesh.
Autumn is here.

Eloise Oldfield (8)
All Saints CE Junior School

Tick-Tock

Tick-tock, tick-tock,
Time to tell a story,
A story of the seasons.

Tick-tock, tick-tock,
Time to see spring flowers,
Spring flowers in the sun.

Tick-tock, tick-tock,
Time to go on holiday,
On holiday we have fun.

Tick-tock, tick-tock,
Time to see the falling leaves,
Falling leaves, red, orange and brown.

Tick-tock, tick-tock,
Time to play in the snow,
Snow, cold and damp.

Tick-tock.

Sam Blackwell (9)
All Saints CE Junior School

Time

Tick-tock, tick-tock,
Time to see the past,
The past of wonders.

Tick-tock, tick-tock,
Time for the present,
The present of now.

Tick-tock, tick-tock,
Time to go to the future,
The future of discovery.

Tim Lees (8)
All Saints CE Junior School

Number Poem

I have a new best friend
And he's the number 0!
He's amazing!
The first time I saw him
Was on the number line
And he was the one in front.
That's how special he is!

When we did the times tables,
$0 \times 1 = 0$ and $0 \times 50 = 0$. *Wow!*
The other day he came round mine,
We did nothing but play on my DS!
When we finished, we had no levels left,
I was ecstatic.

There's lots of words for 0,
Like nothing, zero, naught etc.
The other day my brother did a quiz,
He got 0 right, even $7 \times 0 = 0$!
That's why 0's my best friend!

Samuel Bird (9)
All Saints CE Junior School

Me And You

M uch happiness
E nough for everyone

A round the world we are friends united
N ever walk away
D on't leave friends

Y ou and me
O pen your heart
U nited we are a team.

Emily Davies (8)
All Saints CE Junior School

The Disappearing Senses

(Based on 'The Sound Collector' by Roger McGough)

An odd thing happened to me today,
I couldn't see or hear,
Not even taste a single thing,
Not lager, not even beer.

The smell of melted chocolate did not come to my nose,
Nor it's cooling heat.
Oh, the lovely smell of it,
But no tingle in my feet.

No feel of my gentle skin,
I couldn't kiss my mother's lip,
My dimpled hands, my button nose,
My tea, perhaps another sip.

Then something burst through the door,
A battle droid from the CIS,
Took a shot at me, no harm,
Then he said, 'Take a look at this.'

I dived out the way,
Even though I couldn't see,
He blasted one,
But boy, did that miss me.

Avast, people, I will return.
Then we stood, didn't know what did happen.
Then the droid,
He started to sadden.

All these things have disappeared,
But wait! Look back along the track.
A gust of wind appeared
And brought my senses back.

Chris Merker (11)
All Saints CE Junior School

Number Poem

My favourite number is 10,
I'm ten now.
It's my best friend,
As ten is the best age to be.

Then I found 2 x 10 = 20,
Then 30, then 40, and 10 x 10 = 100.
I found millions, even *billions!*

I bought the best thing ever
Out of ten pounds,
It was a stone carved number 10!
I bet no one, I repeat, no one,
Will love it as much as me.
My eyes started to shimmer
When I saw the glimmering sculpture.

My friend, number 10!

Ellen Drewe (10)
All Saints CE Junior School

Cathedrals - Winchester

W onderful water, secret from sight
 I nteresting images, old origin
N orman nave, fabulous font
C alm crypts, weary waters
H igh windows, halfway to wonder
E xtraordinary statues, eternally still
S uper secret, silent stairs
T owering stars, throughout space
E mbracing seats, enjoyable sights
R eliable river running rapidly.

Will Hooper (9)
All Saints CE Junior School

Number Poem

I went to the airport with 2
we went to the shops
there was one row of shops on one side
and one row of shops on the other side
$1 + 1 = 2$!

When we were on the plane, I saw outside
three birds on the grass then two flew away
then one came back, that equals two
and we sat on two chairs!

When we were in the air I went to get some food
I got one for 2 and one for me, that equals two!
On the way, I saw a man with the number 2 on him
and the food had two bottles of water with it!

We had lots of fun but I'd never go without number 2!

Peter Follett (10)
All Saints CE Junior School

School Years

S pecial students work in class
C ool children play the brass
H appy teachers don't get angry
O ther teachers just get hungry
O utstanding efforts from some children
L earning all the best they can

Y ear by year they learn much more
E xperimenting things never before
A stonishing work from all the best students
R apacious naughty children wreck
S caring everyone around them.

Alysha Taylor (9)
All Saints CE Junior School

Is Pain A Feeling?

(Based on 'The Sound Collector' by Roger McGough)

An odd thing happened to me today,
A misty man came by,
He took all the senses,
Because I couldn't see out my eye.

The shout of the dogs next door
Are as quiet as a mouse,
It's like it never happened,
I'm not sure I'm in my house.

The sight of lovely chocolate cake,
And the lemon, ripe and sweet,
I know there is nothing wrong
With eating a bit of meat.

The feel of me being punched
Has faded in the air,
And the annoying feel of chewing gum
Getting stuck on my chair.

The taste of my mum's fudge
Has all been thrown away,
And the lovely steak my father cooks,
But only in mid-May.

Some of the senses that have disappeared
I miss and have to cry,
But somehow I also hear a shout,
I answer back, well try.

Jordan Luscombe
All Saints CE Junior School

The Senses Whisper

(Based on 'The Sound Collector' by Roger McGough)

An odd thing happened to us today,
A whisper whooshed right past,
Collected every single sense
And left us all aghast.

The smell of fresh cut grass,
The horses running wild,
Day and night watching the stars shine,
The cool breeze so mild.

The touch of a baby's skin,
Warm and soft in winter,
Nothing can stop the snow from falling,
Which will stop a splinter.

My beautiful prom dress
Has disappeared again,
I wonder who has taken it?
Only my little brother, Ben.

The sight of my dad's smiling face,
My mum's sweet perfume,
My gran's cleaning the house,
Running in and out of every room.

The sound of horses neighing,
The clipperty-clop on the yard,
The *thump* as they land from a jump,
Galloping in the fields so fast.

All these things should come back,
I couldn't live without them.
I see him running off,
Escaping to his den.

Rachel Jordan (10)
All Saints CE Junior School

The Senses Whisper

(Based on 'The Sound Collector' by Roger McGough)

An odd thing happened to us today,
A whisper whooshed right past,
Collected every single sense
And left us all aghast.

The smell of freshly made coffee
As I wake up in the morn,
The look of disappointment
As my favourite top is torn.

The touch of my velvet jeans,
Lovely, soft and red,
The lovely smell of jam on toast
As I put it on his head.

The sight of my nan's smiling face
As I run to her and laugh,
Brushing past the pleasant flowers
Lining her garden path.

The sound of songs from music,
Singing rises and falls,
Will I one day be part of that
In magnificent concert halls?

All these things have disappeared,
But wait! Look back along the track.
The whisper has returned once more
And brought the senses back!

Eloise Joy (10)
All Saints CE Junior School

The Senses Gone

(Based on 'The Sound Collector' by Roger McGough)

An unusually weird thing happened,
A cold air rushed right past,
It flew with incredible speed
And left my room last.

It collected all the senses,
The smell of flowers
And home-made cakes,
Then left the cowards.

It collected all the senses,
The taste of apple pie,
The look of disappointment,
The happiness now a lie.

A touch of fur on a dog's back,
Perfect, soft and smooth,
The touch of bark on a crumbled tree,
The leaves gently move.

The sight of my friend's smile
Makes me laugh with joy,
Rushing past all the plants,
Gaining a lovely toy.

The sound of the crowd singing
As I score a perfect goal,
Will I score again
And complete my goal?

All the things disappeared,
But wait! Look at the big red sack,
The cold air has returned
And brought the senses back.

Connor McCabe (11)
All Saints CE Junior School

The Sense Snatcher

(Based on 'The Sound Collector' by Roger McGough)

A strange thing happened to me today,
A shadowy man walked towards our door,
Put every sense into a jar
And muttered something about the law.

The smell of burnt black toast,
Filling the room with smoke,
The look of disappointment
When the telly broke.

The touch of sticky fingers
On my warm arm,
Dried marmalade or jam it was,
I didn't keep calm.

The sound of my brother's rock music,
Drum beats rise and fall,
Will I one day be away from here,
Instead of listening to this drool?

The taste of golden baked rolls,
I've eaten four,
But how many I can eat,
My mum can bake more!

The sight of my dad's smiling face
As I foul him to the floor,
I hope he's not really hurt,
I didn't mean to bore.

All these things have suddenly gone,
The man must have been insane,
But wait! Look out,
The senses are back again!

Thomas Kelly (10)
All Saints CE Junior School

The Senses Whisper

(Inspired by 'The Sound Collector' by Roger McGough)

An odd thing happened to us today,
A whisper whooshed right past,
Collected every single sense
And left us all aghast.

The smell of fresh-cooked burgers
On a beautiful Monday morn,
The look of disappointment
As my favourite jeans are torn.

The touch of fresh-painted walls,
Perfect, smooth and wet,
The ball goes into the net
And wins a dollar bet.

The sight of Chelsea's football pitch,
As I run to it and smile,
Moving towards the club players
As I meet them and laugh.

The sound of beautiful music,
Melodies rise and fall,
Will I one day be part of that
In that magnificent concert hall?

The taste of my mum's pancakes,
My brother's eaten four!
But however many he can eat,
I can manage more.

All these things have disappeared,
But wait! Look back along the track,
The whisper has returned once more
And brought the senses back.

Max Robinson (10)
All Saints CE Junior School

Senses Demon

(Based on 'The Sound Collector' by Roger McGough)

A weird thing happened to me today,
A blizzard whooshed right past,
Trapped every single sense
And left us horrified.

The smell of cut grass
On a beautiful morn,
The look of disappointment
As my favourite jeans are torn.

The touch of a lion's skin,
Perfect, rough and hard,
The dimpled paws,
Heart-shaped nose
And faultless huge feet.

The sight of my friends' smiling faces
As I talk to them and laugh,
Brushing past the vivid trees
Lining the playground path.

The sound of crazy music,
The drumming rise and fall,
Will one day I be part of that
On that extraordinary stage performance?

The senses demon has got it all,
But wait! Look back along the track,
The demon has returned once more
And brought the senses back!

Damien Mony (10)
All Saints CE Junior School

Feeling Strange

(Inspired by 'The Sound Collector' by Roger McGough)

A strange thing happened to me today,
A whisper flew right past,
Every single sense was gone
And it left us all aghast.

The smell of growing flowers
On a lovely warm spring morn,
The look of unhappiness
As my pair of jeans are torn.

The touch of a knobbly tree,
Perfect, rough but sweet,
The rough pointy hands,
But still the birds go tweet.

The sight of my sister's grumpy face
As I skip to her and scream,
Walking past the kitchen table
And squirting her with cream.

The sound of beautiful music
As the orchestra instruments call,
I one day will be part of that,
In that magical music hall.

The taste of my mum's cupcakes,
My sister's eaten four,
But however many she can eat,
I can manage more.

All these senses have disappeared,
But wait, look back along the track,
The thief has returned once more
And brought them all back.

Annabelle Scott (10)
All Saints CE Junior School

Smell Of The Senses

(Inspired by 'The Sound Collector' by Roger McGough)

The strangest thing happened,
A fragrance zoomed straight past,
Snatched every single sense
And ran away so fast.

The feel of my softest blanket
As I wake up in the morn,
The sun begins to shine,
The bright green grass on our lawn.

The smell of greasy sausages
Roams the room all around,
The hungry crying baby
Makes such a wretched sound.

The taste of freshly-squeezed orange
Clears my throat right down,
Don't know what to do today,
Why not make a crown?

As I walk down the stairs
My belly starts to rumble,
'Mum, I'm ever so hungry,'
My mum says, 'Please don't mumble.'

I miss all these senses,
It seems so gloomy and black,
If only when I open the door
They would all come rushing back.

Elsie Sime (11)
All Saints CE Junior School

The Sound Collector

(Inspired by 'The Sound Collector' by Roger McGough)

A weird thing happened to me this morning,
A shiver went right through me
And gathered all my senses
So I couldn't see.

The smell of lovely fresh grass
On a colourful spring morn,
The look of luck
As my favourite jeans were worn.

The touch of silky skin,
My lovely soft and sweet,
The little tiny hands
And minute pink feet.

The sight of my gran's smiling face
As I launch myself to her laugh,
Racing past the vivid flowers
Lining the garden path.

The sound of flowing music,
Melodies rise and fall,
Will I ever be part of this
In the magnificent concert hall?

Georgina Shipman (11)
All Saints CE Junior School

Teamwork

T ogether we care for
E ach other
A greements are made
M anagement is important
W ork together
O pinions are important
R ights, respect, responsibility
K ind and caring.

Natasha Voase (8)
All Saints CE Junior School

Funfair Funky

Fireworks banging,
Speedy rides clanging.

Candyfloss tastes so great,
Like hot dogs on my plate.

Kids' pockets bulging,
Pound notes unfolding.

Toys, toys here and there,
Eager children stop and stare.

Families coming down the streets,
Coming in their massive Jeeps.

Entering the fortune tent,
I wish that I never went.

For you see, she was such a fake,
Said that I lived by the lake.

The helter-skelter goes so high,
You cannot hear the people cry.

Jordan Byrne (8)
All Saints CE Junior School

What Is Silver?

(Based on 'What is Pink?' by Christina Rosetti)

What is silver? The moon is silver,
Shining on a river.

What is grey? A rock is grey,
Sitting on the beach's bay.

What is blue? A river is blue,
Where the fish swim through.

What is red? A cherry is red,
Sitting on the Earth's bed.

What is green? Grass is green,
That we've all seen!

Lavin Deeba (9)
All Saints CE Junior School

Where Have All The Senses Gone?

(Inspired by 'The Sound Collector' by Roger McGough)

A strange wind blew in our town today,
An odd one, yes I'm sure,
Snatched every single sense away
And we could find no cure.

The smell of pancakes cooking,
With maple syrup too,
My sisters sneaking in my room
And the sound of them shouting, 'Boo!'

The touch of water on my face
As I begin to wash,
The feeling of my scratchy soap,
It isn't very posh.

The sight of my hamster, Toffee,
Doing the monkey bars,
I'd better fill her food bowl up,
Otherwise she might starve.

The sound of my favourite music,
Blasting everywhere,
I can even hear it
If I go up the stairs!

The taste of my mum's burgers,
She makes the best in the world,
I can only manage one,
But I'm only a little girl.

We can have these things no more,
But wait! We can bring them back!
The odd thing about this wind
Is that it carries a sack!

Aimee Smith (11)
All Saints CE Junior School

The Sense Thief

(Inspired by 'The Sound Collector' by Roger McGough)

A strange thing happened to us today,
A whisper dashed right past,
Gathered every single sense
And left us all aghast.

The smell of fresh harvest,
Looking at beautiful spring corn,
The look of disappointment
As my greatest trousers are torn.

The touch of black, glossy velvet,
Perfect and great with zeal,
The graceful fur, beauty touch,
And faultless, sweet, good feel.

The sight of my mum's smiling face
As I dash to her and laugh,
Dancing past the vivid flowers
Covering her garden path.

The sound of gracious melodies,
Music rises and falls,
Will I one day be in that room,
In that magnificent royal hall?

The taste of my mum's apple pie,
The one that I adore!
But however many I can eat,
My mum just bakes more!

All these things have simply gone,
But wait! Look back along the track,
The thief at last has come once more
And given our senses back!

Jonathan White (11)
All Saints CE Junior School

Apple

On the table in front of me
I see an apple, chubby and green as can be.
It looks like a leafy green forest.

I carefully extend my slim arm,
Still staying very relaxed.
It feels like a polished surface.

I nervously open my jaws,
It tastes like a mouth-watering sour sweet.
I'm so glad that my mum didn't catch me!

Cori Deverick (11)
All Saints CE Junior School

Lions

Lions stand proud as they rule the jungle,
Like a bodyguard protecting something special,
With their golden coats and tatty manes.
The thumps of their paws echo
As they catch their prey.
Their fierce roars threaten you
As they hit you like a horrible child
And they purr like a motorbike revving up.

Morgan Attwood-Summers (10)
All Saints CE Junior School

Thunder

Thunder rumbles like a furious parent stamping down the corridor.
Thunder bites you like a snake attacking
When you are least expecting.
The rain calms it when an outburst of lightning strikes.
Thunder sounds like a beat on the big bass drum
Ringing vigorously around your ear constantly.
Thunder blocks out the lightning with its shouts of joy!

Ellen Grace O'Hara (10)
All Saints CE Junior School

Crickets

Singing like a golden angel,
Looking on us joyfully.

Hopping rapidly like a hyperactive frog,
Looking for snacks to nip on.

Sleeping calmly like a hibernating owl,
Hooting gently.

Scurrying swiftly like a panic-stricken child,
Running towards a comforting hug.

Crickets are unusual creatures.

Lee Colegate (11)
All Saints CE Junior School

The River

The river is as blue as the midnight sky,
It glistens in the morning sun,
It streams along like an Olympic runner,
The fish hang out down at the bottom.

Twisting and turning at every bend,
It is as gracious as a beautiful flamingo.
The murky water swirls around,
It trickles along like a singing robin.
A river flows on, never stopping.

Matthew Clarke (11)
All Saints CE Junior School

Lightning

Lightning is as sharp as a pointed needle.
It is as quick as a stripy tiger chasing a zebra.
It is as loud as a huge giant roaring all over the world.
It is as bright as a flame on a candle.

Sophie Franklin (11)
All Saints CE Junior School

Blue

If I was a colour I would be blue,
It's the colour of the sea and the sky too.
From the blue sky falls down the calm blue rain,
And the dark blue sea is definitely not plain.
Blue can be the tears from a child's eye,
Or the river that gracefully dances by.

Blue is also like turquoise and green
And the colour that is never not to be seen,
This is the colour that's gentle and never dull,
But an also be extremely powerful.
Blue is water, crystal-clear and pure,
I think it means happiness, though I can't be sure.

Abigail Brooks (10)
All Saints CE Junior School

Eagles

The eagle sits proud on its roost,
Like the Queen of England.
It stares down on the jungle, pride swelling in its chest.
It takes off, its white, marshmallow
Head pointed towards the ground.
The last second, it swoops up into the air
Like a plane taking off from a runway.

The eagle patrols the sky, searching for its prey.
It sees its prey, swoops down, talons extended.
After it has finished hunting, it flies back
To its roost, proud to be what it is.

Matthew James Williams (11)
All Saints CE Junior School

Kitchen Riddle

I'm as greasy as a frog,
As rough as a rock,
As leaky as a drain,
That's how the world sees me.

I spend my time in the sink
With the vegetables and dishes,
Who are teasing, complaining and moaning to each other,
Waiting to be washed.
That's how the world sees me.

But in my dreams
I'm as shiny as metal,
As beautiful as a primrose,
As elegant as a ballet dancer,
Cooking dinner in a famous restaurant,
That's how I'd like to be!

Calum Rainier (8)
All Saints CE Junior School

Water

Water is life,
It can start life and it can end it.
It comes in many forms: rain, sea, pond and lake.
It flows gently, making calm sounds
Like a soft lullaby,
But it can gush and pour angrily
Like a lion, strong and proud.

I like water as rain,
As it trickles down like fairies.
Water has many parts to it, good and bad,
But we must accept both
So we truly understand.

Hayley Bowen (11)
All Saints CE Junior School

A Friend

If you have a friend,
You should treasure it in your heart.
A friend is like a diamond,
Hard to find and lucky to have.

When you find a new friend,
You feel warm inside,
As though you are all wrapped up in a fluffy blanket.

A true friend is someone
Who makes you smile and laugh,
Just like a funny clown
When you're feeling down.

So if you have a true friend,
Make sure you treasure them,
Like a memory you would never forget,
Just as they would treasure you!

Jordan Scott (10)
All Saints CE Junior School

Wind

The wind curves round the corner
Like a carpenter at work.
When it's vicious it seems
To make me shiver and quirk.
It howls like a mournful wolf,
Crying as the wind blows,
It will fly past,
Faster than a car goes.
It livens up my day
Making everything rush by.
By the time it's gone,
I haven't had time to say, 'Hi.'

Samuel James Polden (11)
All Saints CE Junior School

A Poem For All Seasons

Hibernation is over, the rabbits are out to play,
Spring shows a hope of new beginnings,
Days get longer, more time to play,
Flowing rivers creeping through the misty countryside,
Eggs hatch, the chicks poking their heads out to look around,
Squirrels staring around.

School's over! The summer holiday comes before your eyes,
It is getting hotter, now it's time to play cricket,
It is getting lighter, shadows are getting longer,
Sun rises and the sky is getting pinker,
Time of birth.
Suncream selling quickly in the shops.

Hedgehogs and squirrels finding a place to sleep for winter,
The crunchy leaves falling from the trees,
You can feel it getting colder,
Bonfire and Firework Night is coming,
Birds migrate and start their journey to somewhere hot,
Time to wrap up warm again.

Christmas is coming, start to be good,
Children are having a snowball fight,
Time to open those loud Christmas crackers,
Time to get comfy in your bed,
Time to eat Christmas pudding and roast dinners,
Christmas trees and Christmas lights are coming.

Luke Mason (9)
All Saints CE Junior School

Kitchen Riddle

I'm moist like a frog,
As portable as a shoe,
As craggy as a rock,
That's how the world sees me.

I spend my time in the sink
With the bubbles,
Talking about all they have done,
Waiting for a hand to bring a friend,
That's how the world sees me.

But in my dreams
I'm as arid as a desert rock,
As bulky as an elephant,
As level as a sheet of metal,
But exploring the world in a plane,
That's how I'd like to be!

Max Barker (8)
All Saints CE Junior School

Kitchen Riddle

I'm as rigid as titanium,
As hollow as a nostril,
As smooth as paper,
That's how the world sees me.

I spend my time with a noisy restaurant,
The chefs giving me to lots of different people,
That's how the world sees me.

But in my dreams,
I'm as flexible as a hair,
As packed as wood,
As rippled as fur,
That's how I'd like to be!

Joseph Beardsley (8)
All Saints CE Junior School

The Sense Assassin

(Inspired by 'The Sound Collector' by Roger McGough)

A man in black and white
Knocked on the door today,
He shattered all my sense
And sold them on his way!

The sight of my dog's face
As I run to him and play,
Sprinting past my dad
In the massive field today.

The smell of nice hot custard
On a beautiful apple pie,
The look of disappointment
As my favourite teacher says 'bye.

The taste of my brother's cheesecake,
My dad's eaten half,
He's guzzling it down by the second,
He's spilt some on my scarf.

The touch of this assassin,
He would surely feel my fist,
His rough hands and over-large nose,
I'd give his wrist a severe twist.

Oh no, they are gone,
Life will be a bore,
I can't stay up late,
I'll even miss my mum's snore.

Thomas Hunt (10)
All Saints CE Junior School

A Poem For All Seasons

The attractive spring scene breaks through the dullness of winter,
Beautiful, colourful flowers plunge into bloom,
Cheerful, happy children run freely across the green wet grass,
The warm golden sun beats down on me,
The fresh air smothers me like big fluffy pillows,
The temperature warms me outside and inside.

Children merrily look forward to the long, blissful afternoons in
the sun,
The sound of children splashing in the refreshingly cool pools,
As I pick the fresh juicy berries, I am shaded with my pink
summer hat,
Picnics by the crystal blue sea,
Listening to the loud calling seagulls,
Blissful bike rides with the family.

Summer passes quickly away,
Red, yellow, golden leaves fall swiftly to the ground,
Bare, cold trees sway from side to side,
Fun conker fights take place,
Children dress in scary, vile costumes ready for Hallowe'en,
The crackling golden bonfire rises from the ground.

Children and parents dress cosily in warm, layered clothes,
Snow as white as snowy polar bears settles on the ground,
A mug of hot chocolate melts luxuriously in my mouth,
The Christmas tree struggling to be lifted from the loft,
The season of families and friendships,
A time of giving and receiving, fun and laughter.

Isabel Hensby (10)
All Saints CE Junior School

A Poem For All Seasons

Spring is coming and everyone's happy,
The bright new colours of spring everywhere,
Animals are coming out from their hibernation,
With flowers growing, pushing up to the fresh air,
Leaves are blowing in the trees by the noisy wind,
And the rabbits are jumping around on the frosty ground.

The lovely golden sun brightening up the clear blue sky,
The days are getting longer with people knowing it's summer,
Birds are flying in the sky making noisy sounds.
People playing all around,
The flowers are growing in the garden,
With beautiful buzzing sounds.

Leaves are falling from the trees,
Brown, red, orange, green,
Animals are getting ready for their hibernation,
Everybody gathering up their sweets from Hallowe'en,
People can feel it getting colder,
Crunching sounds from the old brown leaves.

Everyone is counting down the days till Christmas,
With the frosty sound of people walking through the snow,
Shouting from the children making snowmen and throwing snowballs,
People dressing up warm for a trip to the ice rink,
The lakes are frozen with coldness on people's feet,
People snuggling up to the fire with blankets around them.

Molly Ryan (9)
All Saints CE Junior School

A Poem For All Seasons

Children playing on long grass, kicking a ball,
Animals coming out of hibernation,
Days are getting longer, more time to play,
Purple and yellow flowers coming to life,
Squirrels climbing trees,
Animals are hunting for food.

The sun getting hotter,
More people coming out to play,
Excited people packing for their holidays,
Birds flying high in the sky,
Animals growing up and getting stronger,
Shouts of joy from people splashing in the sea.

Conkers cracking, hitting each other,
Bonfires roaring, fireworks exploding,
Hallowe'en is scary and creepy,
People stamping on crunchy leaves,
School is starting again,
Animals getting ready for hibernation.

Snow is never coming,
Father Christmas is climbing chimneys,
Days are getting shorter,
Skiing holidays,
Rain is more likely to come,
Christmas tree lights flashing.

Edward Hensby (10)
All Saints CE Junior School

A Poem For All Seasons

Spring colours brightening up to see your eyes,
Hibernation finishing whilst spring is showing hope for
new beginnings,
In the evening the sunset's colours brighten up for beauty,
Chicks hatching to see the colours of spring,
Different colours sprinkled around the place of play,
Time of play.

The summer sun for flowers,
Sun getting hotter, beating on the earth,
Sunset as pink as blossoming flowers,
Sun is getting hotter, shadows are getting hotter,
Children playing around the fields,
Summer is the time for birthdays.

Leaves from the tress of autumn,
Birds vibrating to a beautiful sound,
Conker fights in the playground,
Fires glowing brightly,
Animals preparing for hibernation,
Time for fun.

Fires warming up the centre of your heart,
Christmas presents unopened,
Warm fires glowing,
Hot chocolate warming up your breath,
A time for love and comfort,
Celebrating New Year.

Katriona Holroyd (9)
All Saints CE Junior School

A Poem For All Seasons

Spring popping the winter bubble,
Lambs jumping like a kangaroo that has just been let free,
Frosted ground melting, getting ready for warm, sunny spring,
Walking to a well to get fresh freezing water, ready to drink,
Flowers making people happier,
Children getting ready to play.

Summer holidays, children rushing for a break,
Going on holiday, can't get to sleep the day before you go,
Bright yellow, red, orange sun shining upon your pale face,
Swimming in the warm, light blue sea,
Building sandcastles in the sand, in the scalding sun,
Freezing cold showers cooling you down.

Leaves turn red, yellow, orange and brown,
Hallowe'en, witches saying 'Trick or treat.'
Days getting colder,
Hot cups of tea and coffee and hot chocolate before bed,
Filling up hot water bottles with hot water,
Planting pumpkin seeds,
Jumping in enormous leaf piles.

Snow falling to the white ground,
Snowflakes each with different identities,
Eating boiling hot Christmas pudding,
Building a sledge with your grandparents,
Then flying down a hill on the sledge,
Christmas lights shining in the snow.

Eleanor Leiper (10)
All Saints CE Junior School

A Poem For All Seasons

Scenes getting prettier and really coming alive,
Easter eggs being celebrated as real eggs are hatching,
Flowers popping out making everyone feel happy,
Blossom bursting out, making the new season more special,
The dull winter gone for another year,
The cold, blank winter turning into the colourful, warm spring.

Summer at last is here, making the world more joyful,
Breathtaking heat like none of the other seasons,
Days at the beach, long remembered,
Playing in the paddling pool, what fun!
Fruit growing, such as strawberries and blueberries,
A time for family holidays.

Leaves falling rapidly off the trees,
Bonfires and fireworks lighting up the town,
Animals hibernating as the heat fades away,
Conker fights, the centre of attention,
The beautiful yellow turning into a crispy brown,
Hallowe'en taking over.

Winter, the time of cold and frost,
Snowball fights and snowmen,
The long freezing days leading up to Christmas,
The excitement of staying up till midnight on New Year's Eve,
A time of family get-togethers,
A time for a new beginning.

Sophie Lane (9)
All Saints CE Junior School

A Poem For All Seasons

New flowers blooming into prettiness,
Hibernation is over, rabbits come out to play,
Nights getting brighter, people staying out later,
Dogs rapidly drinking from water bowls,
Children playing in carefree happiness,
April Fool's Day is here.

Sun is getting hotter, beat by beat,
Boys playing football, passing the glowing ball in the sunlight,
The ash-like orange sun turning yellower by the day,
The blue skies cloudless,
Sandy beaches hot on your feet,
People splashing in pools of water.

Birds start to migrate,
The bare trees swaying in the powerful wind,
The spooky sounds of Hallowe'en night,
The hibernation season starts again for animals,
Skies turning greyer and greyer,
Crunchy leaves piled over the unlucky child getting bundled.

Putting up Christmas trees ready for Santa,
Newly fallen snow gleaming freshly,
Warm, cosy fires in the evening,
Thick hot chocolate in Dad's big mug,
Presents under the tree, waiting to be opened,
People sledging after a massive snowfall.

Harry Willis (9)
All Saints CE Junior School

A Poem For All Seasons

Pretty scenes outside your window,
The season of birth,
The evenings getting lighter,
Easter drawing near,
Days getting longer, more time to play,
Eggs crack, chicks poke their heads out to look around.

School's over! The summer holidays have come for the
excited children,
The shadows of the people as the sun beats down on them,
Sports day in the schools,
Time on the beach with the crystal-clear sea,
Suncream selling quickly in the shops,
Paddling pools being got out for the children to play.

Colourful gardens beginning to fade,
Scary costumes being worn on Hallowe'en,
Birds migrate,
Animals get ready for hibernation,
People dive in leaf piles, getting told off by teachers,
Bonfires sending up smoke in people's gardens.

Snow falls, making everything white,
Fires burn, sending smoke up the chimneys,
Children have snowball fights,
Snowmen with carrots as noses, stones as mouths,
Santa delivers presents to each house,
Rudolph's nose shines, leading the way.

Saskia Tyler (10)
All Saints CE Junior School

Snowball Fights

S now flying in the air
N aughty people throwing ice
O ver people's heads the missiles go
W icked sledging down a hill
B oys and girls all having lots of fun
A mazing sights of a pure white blanket
L aunching snow everywhere
L oving every minute of the scene

F iring snowballs from their bases
I llustrated snowmen get made
G leeful people playing and laughing
H appiness fills up the air
T ired people after snowball fights
S culpted angels lying everywhere.

Charlie Jessett (9)
All Saints CE Junior School

Number Poem

My mate is 8,
He is really great,
But he is sometimes late.
He is a great mate.

There are so many things I can do to 8,
I can divide it, times it and even square it.
$4 + 4 = 8$ and $8 \div 2 = 4$.
So many things to do to number 8.

I entered the National Lottery.
Two 4's came out, and a 16,
But the Thunderball was 64 (8 x 8),
And I was really excited when it came.
I might try again on the 8th.
8 is my best mate.

Joshua Cronin (9)
All Saints CE Junior School

What Is White?

(Based on 'What is Pink?' by Christina Rosetti)

What is white? A Westie is white,
Running and playing in the night.

What is red? A rose is red,
Dropping petals in the summer bed.

What is cream? A cat is cream,
Shining in the moonlight's gleam.

What is yellow? A lion is yellow,
Gleaming in the sunshine light.

What is grey? An elephant is grey,
Waiting for some food to eat today.

What is pink? A blossom flower is pink,
On a little tree of pink.

What is brown? Chocolate is brown,
In the middle of the town.

What is purple? A pencil is purple,
Making purple swirls and twirls.

Ellie Morris (9)
All Saints CE Junior School

Gargoyle

G reat and powerful, it patrols the streets
A round the corner it comes
R aging, ravenous, yet wise and cunning
G rowing smaller, gradually eroding
O verhearing humans in the day
Y earning more and more in the sunrise
L onely it feels until the day
E xcellent the gargoyle is.

Alex Keeble (9)
All Saints CE Junior School

At The Funfair

Flashing the light in the moon,
We're getting candyfloss near noon.

Round and round goes the vault,
If I was sick it would be my fault.

Would I like the evil ride?
Would I like the fun slide?

Whirling, twirling like a fairy,
The ghost train's really, really scary.

I love this Friday night,
When the fields are lit with light.

In the Funhouse music booms,
And the rockets go *kaboom!*

In the fields lights glisten and gleam,
On the ghost train everyone goes . . .
Scream!

Connor West (8)
All Saints CE Junior School

Gargoyles

G rey and glorious, staying as stone
A ncient and awful, mighty their mouths
R aw and rugged, their wings widen
G rotesque and gruesome, their teeth tough
O utside they sit on the side
Y ear after year, they fly for freedom
L istening for footsteps, they lie on the floor
E legant carvings, energetic children
S ilent stillness coming from creations.

Beccy Mabin (9)
All Saints CE Junior School

A Kitchen Riddle

I'm as bristly as a hairbrush,
As subdued as a silent night,
As slithery as a snake,
That's how the world sees me.

I spend my time washing pots with
The perplexing rubber gloves,
Spluttering about all of the dirty dishes
Lying on the side,
Waiting for the screaming pots
To finish being scrubbed.
That's how the world sees me.

But in my dreams I'm as smooth as a pebble,
I'm as thunderous as a gorilla,
As chunky as a piece of cheese,
Waiting for a fairy to change me
Into something exciting.
That's how I'd like to be!

Emma Holroyd (7)
All Saints CE Junior School

Cathedrals - Winchester

W onderful Winchester, hidden hideout
 I lluminated bible, illustrated by monks
N ave going on forever
C athedral's crypt, flooded to full
H igh altar, heavenly house
E xciting events
S pire towers high above the rest
T owering columns touching the ceiling
E nter worlds of wonder
R ainbow windows, rising wind.

Sam Wright (9)
All Saints CE Junior School

Kitchen Riddle

I'm as bubbly as soap,
As clear as glass,
As watery as water,
That's how the world sees me.

I spend my time in the cupboard
With the washing up brush,
Moaning about cleaning the dirty dishes,
Waiting for after dinner.
That's how the world sees me.

But in my dreams
I'm as smooth as paper,
As dark as black,
As solid as rock,
Swimming in the lovely cool water.
That's how I'd like to be!

Rebecca Thorne (8)
All Saints CE Junior School

Cathedrals - Winchester

W onderful Winchester, hidden hideout
 I llustrated bible, illuminated beautifully
N ever noisy, always alive
C lassified church, always alerted
H ardly noisy, never high voices
E fficient effort always associated
S ilent mouse scurrying along
T all cathedral, touching carpet
E mpty crypt, embracing space
R esplendent seats, raised ceiling.

Harry Williams (9)
All Saints CE Junior School

Kitchen Riddles

I am as leaky as rain,
As greasy as a frog's leg,
As uneven as jagged wood,
That's how the world sees me.

I spend my time in the sink
With vegetables and dishes,
Boasting and teasing each other
About how useful we are,
Just waiting to be uncovered.

But in my dreams I am
As smooth as a shiny sheet of metal,
As unleaky as a gutter,
As dry as sand,
I would like to be used by the king's best chef
To make dinner, lunch and tea,
That's how I'd like to be!

Thomas Rowe (8)
All Saints CE Junior School

Cathedrals - Winchester

W onderful water, remarkable reflections
 I llustrated, interesting, fancy floor
N ew nave, delightful design
C avernous crypt, cold and curious
H andsome, high altar, carved, curvy
E xtraordinary exhibits, marvellously made
S pecial sights, beautifully bold
T raditional treasury, sparkling sights
E xciting exhibits, fancy floors
R emarkable place, glorious place.

James Rampton (9)
All Saints CE Junior School

Kitchen Riddle

I'm as glittery as glitter,
As clangy as cymbals,
As solid as wood,
That's how the world sees me.

I spend my time by the toaster,
With the pepper and salt pots,
I am moaning about the number of things I have to do,
Waiting to be poured out,
That's how the world sees me.

But in my dreams
I'm as dull as darkness,
As silent as a mouse,
As hollow as a hole,
Wishing to be free,
That's how I'd like to be.

Kathryn Lutley (8)
All Saints CE Junior School

Cathedrals - Winchester

W onderful windows, sunlight shimmering
 I nteresting illustrations, beautiful bibles
N oble nave, long and lined
C urious crypt, grand and graceful
H andsome high altar attracts people
E xcellent emptiness as colours creep to the roof
S ongs sung by clever choirs
T errific tours by superb, smart people
E xciting, extraordinary, marvellous monks
R ocky walls reaching God.

Max Pullen (9)
All Saints CE Junior School

Kitchen Riddle

I'm as stiff as a metal door handle,
As subdued as a silent night,
As slithery as a snake,
That's how the world sees me.

I spend my time in the damp sink
With the washing up gloves,
Grumbling about how many dishes
I have to wash,
Waiting for no more dishes,
That's how the world sees me.

But in my dreams
I'm as smooth as glass,
As thunderous as a gorilla,
As flinty as a chunk of cheese,
Waiting to bathe in a pool of water,
That's how I'd like to be!

Lorna Cook (8)
All Saints CE Junior School

Cathedrals - Winchester

W onderful water, secret from sight
 I lluminated bible, illustrated beautifully
N atural carvings, Normans' name
C reative crypt, cool and cramped
H eavenly altar, always holy
E xcellent exhibits
S ound of organs playing in my ear
T eacher's shout in the crypt echoes loudly
E xcellent windows, colourful and bright
R ed and other colours representing cloaks.

Rebecca Niblett (9)
All Saints CE Junior School

A Kitchen Riddle

I'm as bristly as a feather,
As brushable as a brush,
As rough as a splinter of wood,
That's how the world sees me.

I spend my time next to the washing up tub,
With the soap, towel and washing up liquid,
Waiting to make the dishes or basin sparkly,
That's how the world sees me.

But in my dreams
I'm as smooth as a hairbrush,
Unbrushable as an old broom,
As soft as paper,
Waiting for a fairy that can make me real,
That's how I'd like to be.

Matthew Chapman (8)
All Saints CE Junior School

Cathedrals - Guildford

G lorious windows gracefully pointing westward
U naminously decided under the architect's design
I ndefatigable builders, interested in the build
L udicrous children loving the convenience
D ecorous people dazzled by its personality
F amiliar symbols, formed in a service
O ld designs, only just made desirable
R elatively new, resting in nature
D ense history, desolate in the heart.

Edward Moores (10)
All Saints CE Junior School

The Aliens Have Landed

It was raining gently one twilight in a field,
So quiet and so peaceful,
Tiny insects scuttling beneath the long grass,
It was like this a lot.

A scary series of round objects
Was spinning and falling to the ground,
Some sort of alien creature
Was bound to come out.

There was a half magenta, half solid-purple creature
Coming out of one of the circular objects.
It was *very* big.
What was it?

The creature emerged,
Its head was as large as a London Eye pod!
Its eyes were squished together
To form a pentagon.
It had four green tentacles
And four 'crabbish' claws, all orange and very sharp!

Kieran Barker (11)
All Saints CE Junior School

A Poem Based on 'What is Pink?'

(Based on 'What is Pink?' by Christina Rosetti)

What is blue? A raindrop is blue,
Sinking into me and you.

What is green? A plant is green,
Having fun in the scene.

What is yellow? A lemon is yellow,
Watching his friend play the cello.

Olly Earnshaw (9)
All Saints CE Junior School

A Kitchen Riddle

I'm as sparkly as the stars,
I clank just like chains,
I am made of solid brass,
That's how the world sees me.

I spend my time with the shiny black grill,
I'm moaning that I'm getting cold,
I'm waiting for coffee time
So that I can get hot again,
Now that's how the world sees me.

But in my dreams
I'm as dull as a gloomy night,
I'm as tranquil as a mouse,
I'm as fragile as plumage.
I'm waiting to be discovered
In a five-star coffee shop,
Now that's how I'd like to be!

Francesca Collinson (8)
All Saints CE Junior School

What Is Brown?

(Based on 'What is Pink?' by Christina Rosetti)

What is brown? A leaf is brown
Twirling down to the ground.

What is blue? Water is blue,
With fish flowing through.

What is grey? A rock is grey,
Laying on the beach's bay.

What is white? Paper is white,
When learning to write.

What is red? The chair is red,
To sit down when the teacher said.

James Grice (8)
All Saints CE Junior School

Kitchen Riddle

I'm as minute as a mouse,
As dainty as a piece of tissue paper,
As motionless as a stick,
That's how the world sees me.

I spend my time in a cupboard
With the ketchup and pepper pot,
Moaning because people are always
Tipping me upside down and shaking me,
Waiting for a crack of light to burst in,
That's how the world sees me.

But in my dreams I'm as
Gigantic as a mountain,
As bulky as a rock,
As hasty as a dog,
Waiting for a cook to put me on a table
And use me for fish and chips,
That's how I'd like to be!

Oliver Symons (8)
All Saints CE Junior School

What is Silver?

(Based on 'What is Pink?' by Christina Rosetti)

What is silver? The moon is silver,
Shining on the river.

What is yellow? The sun is yellow,
Listening to kids bellow.

What is gold? A dog is gold,
Big, bright and bold.

What is brown? A ball is brown,
Bouncing up and down.

What is pale? I am pale,
Very bright and not a male.

Emily Leonard (9)
All Saints CE Junior School

A Kitchen Riddle

I'm as bristly as a hairbrush,
Solid like my head,
As smooth as a bowl,
That's how the world sees me.

I spend my time with the dirty dishes
And the washing up,
Listening to the gloves who are
Moaning about the dirty pots.
That's how the world sees me.

But in my dreams
I'm a smooth as a pebble,
As soft as a shiny blanket,
As rough as a rock,
But I'm waiting to stop washing those dirty dishes.
That's how I'd like to be!

Ellen Griffiths (8)
All Saints CE Junior School

What Is Brown?

(Based on 'What is Pink?' by Christina Rosetti)

What is brown? A leaf is brown,
Falling to the ground.

What is grey? A cloud is grey,
Hidden up high today.

What is pink? A rose is pink,
Growing next to the fountain link.

What is violet? A petal is violet,
Beautiful, gleaming twilight.

What is yellow? The sun is yellow,
Beaming the colour mellow.

What is blue? A raindrop is blue,
Sitting on you.

Megan Mulcahy (8)
All Saints CE Junior School

The Blind Lady

What is this life full of colour,
Better than any other?

I really want to see it,
But all I can do is hear it.

Please tell me about colour,
It sounds better than any other.

White is like the scary moon,
Lightning crashing, the world goes *boom!*

Pink is like your pretty hands,
Like burying people in the sand.

Red is like our warming beds,
Where my baby brother sleeps like Ted.

Orange is like the flaming fire,
The flame growing higher and higher.

Brown is like the hideous mud,
Only because we had a flood.

Silver is like the glittering stream,
In the moon, its powerful gleam.

Rainbow is the best of colours,
You and me are the best of lovers.

Leander Rodricks (9)
All Saints CE Junior School

Stones

Black and blue.
            Grey and green,
Nothing new,
            Nothing mean.
Perfectly round,
            Oddly shaped.
Rarely found,
            Always naked.

Jessica Bell-Noad (8)
All Saints CE Junior School

Where Have All The Senses Gone?

(Inspired by 'The Sound Collector' by Roger McGough)

A strange wind blew in our town today,
An odd one, yes I'm sure,
Snatched every single sense away
And we could find no cure.

The smell of pancakes cooking,
With maple syrup too,
My sister sneaking in my room
And the sound of them shouting, 'Boo!'

The touch of water on my face
As I begin to wash,
The feeling of my scratchy soap,
It isn't very posh.

The sight of my hamster, Toffee,
Doing the monkey bars,
I'd better fill her food bowl up,
Otherwise she might starve.

The sound of my favourite music,
Blasting everywhere,
I can even hear it
If I go up the stairs!

The taste of my dad's burgers,
He makes the best in the world,
I can only manage one,
But I'm only a little girl.

We can have these things no more,
But wait! We can bring them back!
The obvious thing about this wind
Is that it carries a sack!

Phoebe Busbridge (10)
All Saints CE Junior School

The Senses Whisper

(Inspired by 'The Sound Collector' by Roger McGough)

A strange thing happened to me today,
A whisper rushed right past me,
Collected every single sense
And left us all aghast.

The smell of warm melted chocolate
On a beautiful warm spring morn,
The look of disappointment
As my favourite jeans are torn.

The touch of a velvet dress,
Perfect, soft and sweet,
The dimpled hands, a button nose
And faultless tiny feet.

The sight of my mum's smiling face
As I run to her and laugh,
Brushing past the beautiful flowers
Lining my garden path.

The sound of Leona Lewis,
Her voice rises and falls,
Will I one day be a part of her
In her magnificent concert hall?

The taste of my mum's cake,
My mum's made four!
But however many she can make,
I can manage more!

All these things have disappeared,
But wait! Look back along the track,
The whisperer has returned once more
And brought the senses back.

Jessica Gollop (11)
All Saints CE Junior School

The Senses Whisper

(Inspired by 'The Sound Collector' by Roger McGough)

An odd thing happened to us today,
A whisper whooshed right past,
Collected every single sense
And left us all aghast.

The smell of fresh cut grass,
On a stunning, warm spring morn,
The look of disappointment
As my best-loved jeans are torn.

The touch of a baby's face,
Perfect, rough and sweet,
The dimpled cheeks, button nose
And mini, tiny feet.

The sight of my nan's smiling face
As I run to her and scream,
Brushing past the vivid flowers
Under the bright sun's beam.

The sound of dreadful music,
Screeches rise and fall,
Will I one day be a part of that
In that magnificent concert hall?

All these things have disappeared,
But wait! Look closely up the path.
The whisper has returned once more
And now it's here to last.

James Boyle & David Cook (10)
All Saints CE Junior School

Haiku

My hamsters are cute,
Although they are now quite old
And their ears are bald!

Abigail Mikowski (8)
All Saints CE Junior School

The Senses Whisper

(Inspired by 'The Sound Collector' by Roger McGough)

An unusual thing happened to us today,
A secret whooshed right past,
Gathered every single sense
And left us all aghast.

The smell of fresh air
On a lovely warm spring morn,
The look of disappointment
As my favourite T-shirt is torn.

The touch of a baby's arms,
Perfect, smooth and sweet,
The dimpled hands, button nose
And faultless, diminutive feet.

The sight of my grandma's features
As I run to her and laugh,
Brushing past the vivid colours,
Walk her garden path.

The sound of lively music,
Melodies rise and fall,
Will I one night be part of that
In the magnificent concert hall?

The taste of my mum's cakes,
My brother's tasted four,
But however thousands he can eat,
I could manage more.

All these things have vanished,
But stop! Look back along the track,
The secret has returned once more
And brought the senses back!

Zoe Bradley (10)
All Saints CE Junior School

A Kitchen Riddle

I'm as steamy as an oven,
As shiny as brass,
I crackle as loud as I can,
That's how the world sees me.

I spend my time by the sink
With the tap running,
I don't like being hot,
That's why I give off steam,
Waiting for my temper to go away,
That's how the world sees me.

But in my dreams
I'm as cold as a dark night,
I'm as dull as dark,
I'm as quiet as a gerbil.
Being poured by the Queen,
The tea sloshing around inside me,
That's how I'd like to be!

Sarah Thornton (8)
All Saints CE Junior School

Fire

The fire blazes angrily like a soaring golden eagle
As he twists and turns upon the breeze.

Crackling like a wicked witch
Plotting yet another evil plot.

The fire dances like a colourful belly dancer,
As she jiggles her shiny bells noisily.

Always be careful with fire,
Make sure it doesn't scorch your back.
Never let a simple flame grow too big for you to handle.

Emily Robinson (11)
All Saints CE Junior School

A Kitchen Riddle

I'm as bristly as a hairbrush,
As dense as a wall,
As smooth as a pebble,
That's how the world sees me.

I spend my time next to the rubber gloves
With the overflowing sink,
Moaning about the dirty dishes,
Waiting for the bowl to be empty,
That's how the world sees me.

But in my dreams
I'm as smooth as a sparkling floor,
As soft as an absorbing sponge,
As rough as a beach full of pebbles,
Waiting for the royal dishes to touch my body,
That's how I'd like to be!

Daisy Hales (8)
All Saints CE Junior School

A Kitchen Riddle

I'm as sandy as the beach,
As minute as an ant,
As rocky as the ground,
That's how the world sees me.

I spend my time next to the
Pepper pot, with the ketchup,
Laughing and waiting for lunch,
That's how the world sees me.

But in my dreams,
I'm as rigid as a pebbly rock,
As enormous as a fat giant,
As soft as a new sofa,
I'd like to have a nice swim in the sea,
That' show I'd like to be!

Elena Mesri (8)
All Saints CE Junior School

Boats - Haiku

Boats go far away
Out to sea they carry gold
Look out for pirates.

Joshua Wright (8)
All Saints CE Junior School

The Rugby Final - Haiku

The ref said, 'No try!'
England are disappointed.
South Africa win!

Sam Amiri (8)
All Saints CE Junior School

My Nan

I miss my nan because
She was very graceful
And she had beautiful eyes.
I miss my nan because
She was very wonderful.
I miss my nan because
She always loved me.

Kelly-May Black (10)
Ashford Hill Primary School

My Grandad

My grandad is as fun as a baby tiger.
My grandad is as fit as a leopard.
My grandad is as strong as a lion.
My grandad is as cool as a movie star.
My grandad is my grandad.

Athina Giles (9)
Ashford Hill Primary School

My Favourite Place

Good times, bad times,
Happy times, sad times.

Warm place, together place,
Open arms, smiling face.

Where I belong, need to stay,
Protected, cared for every day.

Nagged at, shouted at,
All forgiven, forget about that.

Safe place, comfy place,
Longed for loving space.

Tears cried, eyes dried,
Somewhere to run, somewhere to hide.

Wanted, remembered, proud of me,
This is my favourite place to be . . .
Home!

Katie Victoria Lobo (10)
Ashford Hill Primary School

Horse And Cart

'I wrapped my cart nice and warm in its bed.'
She locked me in the lorry.
'I look after my cart.'
She got me all muddy.
'My cart is in good condition.'
I have a broken wheel.
'I care for my cart.'
She poisoned me.
'I pull my cart.'
You left me to get run over.

Daniella Butler (8)
Ashford Hill Primary School

My Dog, Rockey

I long to see my Rockey again,
I long to see my Rockey again,
I long to see my Rockey again,
With two big brown eyes,
I long to see my Rockey again,
He's burnt into my mind,
With his fluffy coat,
His droopy ears,
I just long for him to brush away my tears.
I long to see my Rockey again,
So soft, brown and black,
I long to see my Rockey again,
But I know he can't come back.
I long to see my Rockey again,
With his soft, gentle little pads.
He was gone on Thursday
And I know he can never, ever come back.

Bethany Leah Rain (9)
Ashford Hill Primary School

Love

Dear Love,

I just wanted to say . . .
You brighten up my day
In every way.
When I get up you start straight away,
You never have a holiday.
Every day is like a birthday,
So thank you, Love.

Kayleigh Claire Wickenden (8)
Ashford Hill Primary School

The Bullies

Smack!
Slam!
Kick!
Punch!
They were on me again.
Smack!
Slam!
Kick!
Punch!
They left me in pain.
Smack!
Slam!
Kick!
Punch!
They stole my pencil case.
Smack!
Slam!
Kick!
Punch!
They find me in every place!

Gregory Adam (10)
Ashford Hill Primary School

America

I long to be there,
The wind in my hair,
The sun in my face,
I always wish to be in this special place.

I miss hearing the dolphins splashing in the water,
I miss swimming in the sea,
All I want is to be there
With my mother, father, sister, brother and me.

Heather Smyth (9)
Ashford Hill Primary School

Spain

The sun in Spain
Which is warm on my face,
Reminds me that it's a happy place.

The sea is crystal-blue,
It shines in the sun,
I love to jump and swim in it
And have a lot of fun.

We lay on the sand
At the water's edge,
It flows through my toes,
And a big wave goes up my nose.

I feel so happy
When I'm in Spain
And I hope I will
Go there again.

Molly Lawrence (8)
Ashford Hill Primary School

War

'Blow up that forest depot, private.'
'Can't Sir.'
'Why not?'
'Out of charges, Sir.'
'Get some more from the forest depot'
'Can't Sir.'
'Why not?'
'Blown up, Sir.'
'OK, drive that tank, Private.'
'Can't Sir.'
'Why not?'
'I don't have a driving licence.'

Brandon Collins (9)
Ashford Hill Primary School

Letter To The Army

Dear Army,

I just wanted to say
You are very brave
Fighting every day.
A bullet fired from your gun,
It goes out the end,
Hitting everyone.
Going out to help the poor,
Then travelling back,
And out again, back to war.

Love from,
A person who would like to join.

Callum Hall (10)
Ashford Hill Primary School

Disagreement

'I love my car.'
He locks me in the garage.
'I always pay the bill.'
He stole me!
'I always obey the speed limit.'
He sped down the highway.
'I always take care of my car.'
He drove me into a tree!
'I have twelve points on my licence.'
He's been booked!
'So that's my car.'
He's in court tomorrow!

Samuel Maya (9)
Ashford Hill Primary School

Midwinter's Night

In the midwinter's night,
Go to bed,
Snuggle up tight.
In the midwinter's night,
All is calm in the midwinter's sky.
Look out the window,
Look up high
At all the stars in the sky,
Glimmering, shimmering, they shine,
I pick one from the sky,
It's mine,
I hold it tight.
So I say
In the midwinter's night,
I kiss it,
Then it floats away.
I already miss it.
Then I snuggle down
And go to sleep.

Holly Olivia Hathaway (8)
Ashford Hill Primary School

My Mum

I love my mum,
She washes my clothes,
Makes my dinner,
Takes me out when I'm good,
Gives me hugs and kisses,
Gives me treats,
Never annoying (only sometimes),
Kisses me goodnight when I go to bed,
I love my mum and I always will.

Rebecca Quelch (9)
Ashford Hill Primary School

Something In My Wardrobe

There's something in my wardrobe,
It's been there all day.
It keeps on making funny noises
And it will not go away.

I asked my mother to go and look
But she said everything was all right.
This morning it made a loud squeaky sound
And gave me a rather big fright.

Now I'm venturing in,
I know it will give me a big scare.
So I look inside and there it is,
My tattered, torn teddy bear.

I figured out why it was so loud,
Things were falling on the squeak inside,
But the thing that made the loudest squeak
Was a picture of boats and the tide.

Georgia Martin-Smythe (9)
Ashford Hill Primary School

My Magic Box

(Inspired by 'Magic Box' by Kit Wright)

In my box lies . . .
The sweet smell of spring on a Sunday morning,
The sunset hour on a blood-red sky,
And the salty taste of cheap chips from down the road.

When I open my box I hear . . .
A baby's first laugh when they awake,
The birds calling from silver birch treetops,
And the scattered *pitter-patter* of raindrops on a grimy window.

Inside my box you'll find . . .
The frost gathered, as if in a meeting, on a car's windscreen,
The crisp air on an autumn night,
The love from a mother to her son.

Elliott Robinson (10)
Craneswater Junior School

In My Magic Box . . .

(Inspired by 'Magic Box' by Kit Wright)

In my magic box . . .
I find a flying carpet
With tassels that change colour every now and then.

In my magic box . . .
I see an innocent new smile
On a baby's face.

In my magic box . . .
I find a fairy
Tiptoeing across a bright rainbow.

In my magic box . . .
I see a monkey
Swinging through the trees.

In my magic box . . .
I find on top, butterfly hinges
That fly away and sit back in their place again.

In my magic box . . .
I see a poet
Whose pen flows with ink
And brings great words to the page.

Jessica Wall (11)
Craneswater Junior School

My Hamster

My hamster is my special friend,
A friend in many ways,
Sharing love and companionship,
Just looking for praise.

The clever things she does
Bring a smile to my face,
So to her I dedicate
This small, special place.

Louise Gordon (9)
Craneswater Junior School

The Bear King

Long ago in the land of bears
The old king was ailing,
Law and order in the land was failing.
To add to this tale of woe, a band of hunters was on the go.
'This cannot continue,' said a bear called Joe.
The situation could not be worse.

Together with a band of friends,
He hatched a plan to make amends.
They waited 'til the hunters slept,
Then amongst their bodies quietly crept,
Gathering weapons as they went,
And bundling the sleepers in a sack.

Proceeding to a leafy dell
They threw them down a well.
News arrived that the king was dead.
'We need a leader,' said a bear called Fred.
Stepping forward royally, Joe, the bear, declared
That he got rid of the hunters,
So he would be king.
'The old king is dead, long live the new king.'

Freya Noble (10)
Craneswater Junior School

Dream Land!

All together the trees sway as the wind blows,
The leaves gently land on the ground.
The sun shining on all of the trees around the park.
That's my dreamland.

Beautiful butterflies flying in one big group.
Instead of apples, sweets and roses
Hang off every branch.
Oh what a lovely place it is,
That's my dreamland.

Millie Garside (9)
Craneswater Junior School

My Library

My bookshelf reaches from the ceiling to the floor,
It is crammed full of books but I keep buying more.
From Harry Potter to Horrible Histories,
From old baby books to sinister mysteries.
From Tracy Beaker by Jacqueline Wilson,
To The Famous Five by Enid Blyton.
From books that were made into films,
To films that were made into a book,
It's on the shelf if you take a look.
My favourite books are full of shocks and scares,
But I don't read them at bedtime in case I get nightmares.
Books are great,
Books are fun,
So turn off the television and pick up one!

Jessica Palmer (10)
Craneswater Junior School

The Sister Poem

There may be twelve years between me and my sister
And we argue like a Mrs and Mr,
We will always be together, for ever and ever,
I want to be like her as she is so clever.
She is my best friend, as well as my sister.
Me and my sister,
Sometimes we bicker
Over the TV flicker.
I would never change the love we share,
Because wherever she is, I'll always care.
She is the bestest sister I could ever wish for,
We will be together for evermore.
My sister.

Kirsty Broadway (9)
Craneswater Junior School

When I'm Asleep

When I'm asleep I visit a land
Where I am as small as the palm of your hand,
Where pigs can fly with fluffy wings,
Magical mermaids dance and sing.
The sky is as blue as the deepest sea,
The mountains as high as they can be.
Elephants jump on pogo-sticks,
Cheeky monkeys play their naughty tricks.
Tall trees are covered in sweets and cake,
Busy gingerbread men cook and bake.
The air is full of a lovely smell,
There are lots of stories I could tell.
When I wake I think of that place
And always have a smile on my face.

Amy Johnson (9)
Craneswater Junior School

Penguins

Penguins live in the snow and ice,
I think penguins are really nice.

They lay one egg and keep it warm,
Until the baby chick is born.

Baby penguins are small and fluffy,
When they are scared, they go all puffy.

Grown-up penguins are black and sleek,
With a white tummy and a long black beak.

I think penguins look really funny
When they waddle along or slide on their tummy.

Penguins live in the snow and ice,
I think penguins are really nice.

Isobel Terry (8)
Craneswater Junior School

Our World

The world is here
For the human race,
Hoping to win first place.

The world is floating
In outer space,
Does it have a smiley face?

The world is a neighbour,
Both young and old,
That's what we've been told.

The world is next
To Mercury, Venus and Mars,
It's surrounded by a blanket of stars.

The world is here
For you and for me,
Don't spoil it with greed.

The world is blessed with
Blue oceans and many seas,
They don't want oil spills
To make animals ill.

The world is being
Destroyed by you and I
And often asks, 'Why, why, why?'

The world is losing
Fields of green
And would love them to be seen
For our future generation.

The world is spinning
On an invisible axis,
It wants us to use
More buses, taxis
And *not* our cars.

The world is wanting us
To have fresh air and sun,
For us to play and have some fun.

The world is here
For you and I,
The ozone is damaged
And you know why!

The world wants us
To recycle more,
To help those countries that are poor.

The world can be a lovely place,
It can also be as lonely as space.
Trees help us all to breathe,
So please replace.

Do not be greedy,
Look after our world.

Emily Nagel (11)
Craneswater Junior School

The Dragon . . .

Adamant beast,
Bone picker,
Flesh cruncher,
Blood licker,
Flame flicker,
Ash maker,
Earth shaker,
Widow maker,
Knee quaker,
Egg layer,
Man slayer,
Scaled skyscraper,
King of the skies.

Eoghan D'All (11)
Craneswater Junior School

I Remember

Tasting the crumbly croissant as it struggles away from my mouth,
Tasting the oozing doughnut as I savour it
While licking my sugar-coated lips,
Tasting the fizzy lemonade as the bubbles
Tickle my dehydrated throat,
Tasting the mushy peas and pulling a face in disgust
As they dribble slowly into my stomach.

Looking at the postbox-red London buses
As they scuttle through busy streets like beetles,
Looking at the mighty elephant as it plods
Through the dense, dark foliage,
Looking at the endless starry universe as I peer
Thoughtfully through my tremendous telescope,
Looking at a graceful golden giraffe as it chomps
On the greenest possible leaf it could find.

Hearing the squealing children as they ride
The head-spinning roller coaster recklessly,
Hearing the noisy monstrosity of a motorbike
As it hurtles down the dusty highway,
Hearing the hunting of owls as they tu-whit tu-whoo
Back and forth through the silent night sky.

Smelling the burning bacon as it shrivels and
Blackens on my father's barbecue,
Smelling the pine-scented branches of
Our new Christmas tree while we delicately decorate it,
Smelling the unmistakable aroma of freshly baked bread
As it peeps round the oven door.

Touching the patterned, bumpy tortoise shell
As it trudged grumpily across the freshly-mown grass,
Touching the slimy silver slug as it sticks
To the washed window like a limpet,
Touching the silky softness of my curious ginger cat
As it overlooks the robins feeding,
Touching the jagged rocks as I hesitantly clamber
Up the cliff of my favourite beach.

Noah Clements (10)
Craneswater Junior School

The Spy Who Saves The World

I would like to be a spy
And catch people out with my beady eyes
And use all types of special gadgets,
The way they work, they look like magic!
Earpieces and lasers are my special tools,
With my sunglasses and clothes, I look really cool.

Running or jumping, I really don't care,
When I'm on a mission I could fly through the air!
I catch all the bad guys and work with my team,
Together we are faster than a laser beam.
My family and friends, they don't really know
That I am undercover and sometimes I have to go.

So if you are ever in trouble, just dial 'one',
And me and my team will soon come.
So now you know my little secret
I hope you have enjoyed it, and I hope you keep it!

Joshua Gillmore   (9)
Craneswater Junior School

When I'm Older . . .

I will venture into the obese Sahara sandpit and experience its
                                            miracle mirages,
I will run my own business in its sea of chaos.
I will sail in a galleon and let it wander while I bounce on
                                            its trampoline.
I will soar like an elegant fairy down from a jet plane while it
                                            watches me glide.
I will perfectly perform and see the smiling beams burst out.
I will create a book that will grasp me into its fantasy.
I will speak fluent French like my mother feeding it to me.
I will construct a tower as tall as my ambition,
When I'm older.

Jessica Nickerson   (11)
Craneswater Junior School

My Magic Box
(Inspired by 'Magic Box' by Kit Wright)

In my magic box I will put . . .
A baby's first smile,
An elephant's trunk,
A crocodile's scales
And a boat that has sunk.

A shiny new car,
A jack-in-the-box,
A great white shark's fin
And a fox's red socks.

A ship's pure white sails,
A kitty-cat's paws,
A smooth chocolate bar
And a tiger's sharp claws.

My magic box is bright blue
With happy stars on the lid,
Golden hinges
And memories in the corners.

Molly Hipkin (10)
Craneswater Junior School

My Dog, Ben

My dog, Ben,
Is a shiny black Lab,
He runs and plays
And we think he's fab.

We take him to the beach
Where he has lots of fun,
Swimming in the sea,
Splashing everyone.

We give him treats
When he is good.

Beth Linford (7)
Craneswater Junior School

The Campervan

The end destination will be St Ives,
Where natural beauty always thrives.
A childhood dream we hope to find,
Around the lanes we will wind.

The van chugs on,
On and on.

We head for the New Forest,
This location may well be the best.
We hope to toast marshmallows on the fire,
The glowing treat we admire.

The van chugs on.
On and on.

We roll on to the surf and sea,
It's the place we want to be.
We dream of riding the waves
And pray we don't end up in the caves.

The van chugs on,
On and on.

We finally reach our destination
And succumb to our temptation.
That's hot chocolate, pasties and ice cream,
The delight at which we scream.

The van has come to a rest,
Which, at its age, it likes best.

Marina Sealey (11)
Craneswater Junior School

The Dinosaurs Poem

Dinosaurs are fierce,
Dinosaurs are strong,
Dinosaurs are old
But they really pong.

Dinosaurs are hairy
But they're really scary.

Dinosaur's are different colours,
Red, green, yellow or brown,
But just do not frown
In case they live in your town.

Dinosaurs live around the world,
Dinosaurs are very, very cold.

Dinosaurs are very fun,
Even if they bite your thumb.

George Green (8)
Craneswater Junior School

My Dog, George

George is my dog,
He's better than a frog.
He catches the ball
And runs down the hall.
He plays with his mates
Who get into states.
He lies about his food,
We think he's rather rude.
He plays in the park,
Sometimes in the dark.
He goes in the sea,
Then he has tea.
I love him to bits
But George never sits!

Sophie Nickerson (10)
Craneswater Junior School

Ten Year 4 Children

Ten Year 4 children
Warming up on the line, one fell down
Then there were nine.
Nine Year 4 children
Running to school, one was late
Then there were eight.
Eight Year 4 children
Jogging on the spot, one thought he was in Heaven
Then there were seven.
Seven Year 4 children
Jumping around, one did the splits, needed to be fixed
Then there were six.
Six Year 4 children
Standing next to the swimming pool, one went to dive
Then there were five.
Five Year 4 children
Going on a tour, one got lost
Then there were four.
Four Year 4 children
Standing in jail, one got free
Then there were three.
Three Year 4 children
Eating lunch, one needed the loo
Then there were two.
Two Year 4 children
Lying on the beach, one got burned by the sun
Then there was one.
One Year 4 child
One lonely sad kid got taken by a hero
Then there was zero.

Fatima Khatun (9)
Craneswater Junior School

I Hate!

I hate smelling burnt toast.
I hate smelling petrol in the station.
I hate smelling the cheese coming out of the fridge.

I hate seeming my homework being handed out.
I hate seeing my blood when I hurt myself.
I hate seeing my little sister feel sick.

I hate tasting the sauce on my plate.
I hate tasting the jam on my toast.
I hate tasting chicken fat in my mouth.

I hate hearing my TV so loud.
I hate hearing the bristles on my toothbrush.

I hate touching the dust on the wall.
I hate touching cats' fur.

Gurdit Singh Digpal (10)
Craneswater Junior School

Magic Box

(Based on 'Magic Box' by Kit Wright)

I will put in my magic box . . .
Swaying palm trees in the wind,
The waves of the sea just touching my toes whilst I sunbathe,
And the gentle wind blowing through my hair.

I will put in my magic box . . .
Children chanting for ice cream at the funfair,
People screaming whilst going on roller coasters.

I will surf in my box throughout the ocean wide,
And fly up in the clouds and meet the fairies.

I will also put in my box
My teddies I snuggle up with every night.

Monica Boulton (10)
Craneswater Junior School

Seasons

Winter, autumn, summer and spring,
Altogether they will bring . . .
Happiness, sadness, excitement and madness,
Makes you want to dance and sing.

Autumn lay and watched the leaves fall,
Thinking everyone was so mean and cruel,
Except for one who he thought was great,
Spring, who was his best mate.

Winter stood in the dull, cold sky,
Saw the sun and said goodbye.
He let the rain trickle down,
Making everyone sad and frown.

Spring sat looking at the sun,
Wanting to have so much fun.
She watched the plants and animals grow,
Looking a the chicks' feathers shine and glow.

Summer skipped with a happy face,
Keeping a slow and steady pace.
She's always so pleasant, so cosy and so kind,
But her sun can almost make you blind.

Now you've met all the seasons,
So when you get mad you have your reasons.
Some are good and some are bad
But in the end I know you're glad.

Karamjot Kaur (10)
Craneswater Junior School

Homework

Our homework this week was to write
A poem that sounds really nice
For Little Laureates, two thousand and eight,
A poem we were asked to write.

But it wouldn't come out right
Though I tried nearly all night,
I really want it to be done,
Or playtime will be no fun,
If I have to stay in and write.

And so, I finally declare,
The end of my poem, so there!
I feel I ought to win,
So I'll enter in
My poem which is past compare.

Alice Kellam (10)
Craneswater Junior School

Alone In The Forest

When you're alone in the forest and it gets dark,
It really is no trip to the park.
Howling wind through the trees,
Screeching birds and stinging bees.

No drink or food
And a toilet that's rude.
If no one can find you,
What will you do?

With animals that roar
And creepy-crawlies on the floor,
You're in for a fright
And a very cold night.

Terrianne Carter (9)
Craneswater Junior School

My Sisters

The flashing torchlight wakes me,
The gloe bear flickers in the dark,
I wish I had my own room!

As they practise their dancing,
Singing in time (not!)
I want some peace and quiet!

The channel choice
We can never agree.
Mum switches it off!

But when we swim together,
We have loads of fun.
I do quite like my sisters.

Amina Souhaid (9)
Craneswater Junior School

Swimming Pool

Splashing, crashing and Geronimo,
Bubbles racing up my tummy.
Jumping in the pool is lots of fun,
But remember not to run.

Shouting, screaming and laughter,
Sounds filling up my ears,
Splashing water at each other,
People swimming with each other.

Under water it's very slushy,
With legs kicking everywhere.
Be careful what you do in the pool
Or the lifeguard will blow his whistle.

Josh Tuck (9)
Craneswater Junior School

The Dragon

In sunless caverns, dark and deep,
Ancient dragons lie asleep
On gleaming gold, a greater horde
Than richest kingdoms can afford.

But woe the thief who dares to touch
Coin or ring or chain or such!
However small the thing he takes,
The guardian dragon still awakes.

In fierce pursuit he leaves his lair
And hurtles through the midnight air
And people watching from afar
Cry, 'Look! Oh look! A shooting star!'

From his tongue leaps furious fire
As he glides above, getting higher and higher.
He thinks to himself about this sinner,
He thinks, *I'll have him for my dinner.*

The dragon swoops and lands on a shop
And as you can imagine, the whole thing drops.
He knows he flies like Peter Pan,
But he is still going to eat that man!

But God looks down from his heavenly hide
And says, 'Maybe I should help that guy,
For I *am* God and The Supreme,
And on dragons I'm not too keen.'

So it is not as you think
How all dragons became extinct.
But some day, though I don't now when,
The dragon race shall fly again.

Gloria Truscott (10)
Craneswater Junior School

The Second World War

In the Second World War
Britain scored,
But it was not a happy affair.
Although some people
Met their deaths,
Hitler did not care.

Children were
Sent away for many days
That turned into months,
Then years.

As the years
Went by,
The children sighed
And wished they
Were at home.

But in 1945
Peace arrived
And brought
The children home.

The excited children
Came home
On the train,
So thrilled to find
Their mums and
Dads again.

Sofaya Looker-Ere (7)
Craneswater Junior School

Love

Love is a symbol of life,
Love can bend and break,
Love is wonderful,
Love, you can trust,
Love is like a glowing candle,
Love is romantic,
Love, you can believe in.

Ruby Lepora (7)
Craneswater Junior School

Grass

Grass that tickles my toes,
Magic ran through them when I rose.
Grass sways in the breeze
Like a hundred dancers.
Grass is a hundred colours.
Grass is the everlasting survivor.

Millie Lepora (9)
Craneswater Junior School

Pepper

I love my cat,
He is black and white.
He sleeps all day
And plays all night.
I love my cat, Pepper.

Jordan Grattan (7)
Craneswater Junior School

Treasure

Pirates came into the bay
As an old man on the beach just lay.
They were coming for the treasure
And we had much pleasure
To use it every day.

They rowed ashore and beat up the guards,
Climbed the mountain then played charades.
Suddenly, a man who was very posh
Said, 'Go away, don't you wash?'

They got to the box but it was empty,
But there was actually plenty,
But they could not see it at all.

For the treasure was everywhere,
It was love,
But the pirates did not care.

Joseph Laithwaite (11)
Craneswater Junior School

My Magic Box

(Inspired by 'Magic Box' by Kit Wright)

It's a beautiful day
And I am about to play.
In my magic box I put a feather
Which can tell the weather.

I have a bag full of gold
And I don't care
That my hands
Are cold.

I am running in the rain
And I am ignoring the pain.
Off I go to the shops
To buy some gloves and socks.

Samantha Mapulango Dimingo (8)
Craneswater Junior School

Portsmouth

I can see the Spinnaker Tower pointed up
Like a giant fish bone sticking out from the ground.
I can see the wild waves of Southsea crash against the rocks.
I can see excited children playing as I wander through the park.

I can smell the uncomforting waft of cigarette ashes
Shoot through the air like a thousand pins.
I can smell the fresh sea air as I charge towards the salty water.
I can smell the newly-baked food as I rush across Gunwharf
Sticking my head round every restaurant door.

I can feel the warm, soft fur of dogs as they dash across the park.
I can feel the coldness of ice on a winter's morning
As I scrape it off the car windows.
I can feel the sharp pebbles beneath my feet
As I stumble across the beach.

Megan Linford (10)
Craneswater Junior School

Magic Box

(Inspired by 'Magic Box' by Kit Wright)

I will put in my box . . .
The first smile of a baby,
A bright, shining, full moon sleeping with the sky,
A crunchy, crackling cookie cooking in a cooker.

I will put in my box . . .
The flame of a firework flying in the dark blue sky,
The puff of a deadly dragon's breath,
The skin of a slimy snake slithering along.

I will swim with my box to the ocean's heart
And peer at the golden treasure floating across the sea.
I will talk to the fish for directions back home,
Then fly across skies of wonder,
Then swoop down to Portsmouth, my home city.

Jamshed Gafarov (9)
Craneswater Junior School

My Baby Brother

My baby brother is fifteen months old.
Soft, brown, fluffy hair,
Curly at the back.
Beautiful big blue eyes,
Cheeky little grin,
Eight tiny milky-white teeth,
Weeny little shoes,
A bundle of mischief,
He's always up to tricks,
Like emptying the bin
And resetting the washing machine,
Tearing tissues into tiny bits.
He always wants what we've got,
Loves to dance and kick a ball,
Gives big wet kisses,
Splashes us in the bath,
Pulls faces and makes us laugh.
I love him so much,
My baby brother.

Hanley Morgan (8)
Craneswater Junior School

Miki's 'It's A Secret But!'

It's a secret but my guinea pigs can do cartwheels.
It's a secret but my dad eats twenty-five Brussels sprouts!
It's a secret but my fish has legs.
It's a secret but Mia turns into a cat!
It's a secret but my mum is an alien!
It's a secret but I am a part-time pop star!
It's a secret but I can travel back in time!
It's a secret but sometimes I make things up!

Miki Ginns (8)
Craneswater Junior School

My Magic Box

I've got a magic box
Hidden deep inside my drawer,
It's a very special place
Where mystic dragons soar.

It's a place of mysteries,
Where splendid secrets keep,
It's a place of monsters
Where no one dares to peep.

It's a home of total madness,
A place where no one's been,
Where horses gallop and mice squeak,
A place where unearthly things are seen.

Thanks for listening to my poem so far,
Now I have to put it on hold,
There are more tales about my box
That are waiting to be told . . .

Nicole Poore (11)
Craneswater Junior School

A Winter Walk In The Woods

Wellies squelching in the mud,
Slimy, thick and oozy.

Gloves grabbing rough bark,
Scratchy, smooth and prickly.

Children running down the path,
Falling, tripping, squealing.

Families climbing over rocks,
Stumbling, falling, laughing.

Jacob Thomas (7)
Craneswater Junior School

The Earth Is My Ball

The Earth is my ball, my moon, my stars,
Scattered across the sky.
My dark, my light - my day, my night,
My guiding light throughout my life.

The Earth is my ball, my home, my school,
The place with the people I trust.
My friends, my family - my goodies, my baddies,
All the people for whom I care.

The Earth is my ball, my pen, my paper,
The ink which I use to write.
My black, my red - my nibs, my lead,
Are important things for all.

The Earth is my ball, my you, my me,
All the people in our country.
The nurses, the policemen - the people who help them,
We all make the Earth together.

Emily Hall (11)
Gomer Junior School

TV

When I watch TV
I'm sucked into a world of imagination.

Horror, action and fantasy,
Until my brother takes the remote.

'I wanna watch Boobah,' he cries.
'No!' I shout, *click* goes the remote.

I snatch it back, I say calmly, 'Killer Zombies!'
He screams . . .

Then Dad comes in.

Alex Clements (11)
Gomer Junior School

Hunger

H urt you do as my tummy slowly becomes dark and empty.
U nder my skin you eat up my insides until nothing is left,
  apart from emptiness.
N ever do you leave me alone, you're always there, stalking me,
  laughing at me noisily.
G rowling within me, the pains twist and turn around my body,
  making it unbearable to move.
E mpty cupboards, no food in sight, just as they have been
  for weeks.
R aid me at night, the pains never go away, I cry myself to sleep
  then wake with the same awful pains.

Katie Walters (11)
Gomer Junior School

Silence

S talking, waiting to pounce
I solating words
L eaving out laughter
E very trace of noise is gone, empty
N ot a whisper can be heard
C reeping into my ears
E verything is lonely.

Elizabeth Steer (11)
Gomer Junior School

Happiness

Happiness is a glittery, colourful rainbow.
Happiness sounds like a thousand blissful cheers.
Happiness is the smell of adorable, radiant flowers.
Happiness looks like a million cheery smiles.
Happiness tastes like a huge bowl of scrummy, yummy, brightly-
                                    coloured cherries.

Lauren Mose (10)
Gomer Junior School

Music

Your sweet voice lowers me in and lets me out of my shell,
All my thoughts drift away when you are around.
Your velvet lips kiss my ears gently,
Hypnotising me, slowly putting me in a trance.

I feel I can fly when you start up your beat,
You make me happy when I can't go out and play.
You're a flurry of colour spinning this way and that in my mind,
I can't get you out of my head.

Always putting a huge smile on my face,
The happiness in my eyes grows and grows.
You shall never die, you're immortal it's true,
Always laying somewhere in our colossal world, making a
child cheerful.

We always hear you beating away, following me round all day.
I know you have lots of moods,
Sometimes you're bitter, sometimes you're sad,
But I still love you always, forever.

Natasha Barker (11)
Gomer Junior School

Anxiety

Why, why, why are you so spiteful?
Why are your butterflies constantly taking to the air
In my bone prison trying to get out?
Your tormenting behaviour creeps up on me again and again.
You drench my hands with fear and
Send an army of shivers down my spine.
Beads of sweat drip down my forehead,
I know you sent them.
You torture me with everlasting worry, clogging up my brain.
Why are you so demanding?

Genevieve Norris (11)
Gomer Junior School

Valentine's Day

I had a secret crush one day,
To be exact, the middle of May.
This boy is very tall and thin,
But not as skinny as a pin,
He runs on two feet, but as fast as a cheetah,
In fact he could always beat ya.
Whenever I see him I seem to scream,
His face is as soft as whippy cream.

It was Valentine's Day
When he asked me to come and play,
But instead he took me somewhere else,
We ran and passed Mrs Nelse.

So now he had taken me to this place
But he looked like a tomato 'cause of his face.
He asked me to go out with him,
Suddenly my voice went fairly dim,
Then I shouted, 'Yes! Yes! Yes!'
I was probably overreacting, I guess.

So that was the end of Valentine's Day,
Me and him are in love today.

No I'm not telling you his name!

Katie Bird (10)
Gomer Junior School

Excitement

The joy of the funfair,
The thrill of the lights,
The excitement of the carousel and the horses,
But they also bring fright.
The smell of the candyfloss,
The sound of the clowns,
Excitement, I love your rides,
You'll bring happiness for evermore.

Hayley Westmorland (10)
Gomer Junior School

War

Digs into your heart
Slowly but surely will tear you apart,
Lasts for months, years on end,
So long,
Too long,
When it all ends you think, *why?*
The towns, the lives, the homes too,
All for who should take a crown.

The world now stands dark and dismal,
Empires lay ruined and wrecked.
Emerald forests burnt to the ground,
Beautiful glades, slashed with blades.
Why? I think again, *why did all those people die?*
I beg for a new start,
But no, the end has come,
Not begun.

Connor Powell (11)
Gomer Junior School

Scarlet Tanager

Scarlet Tanager of the sky,
Singing softly a lullaby,
What immortal hand or eye
Can catch your beauty in the sky?

In the distant deeps or skies,
Burnt the fire of thy feathers,
Flying swiftly through the heathers.

And on your beak the sun does shine,
So sweet, so merry and so divine,
Against your cousins, the finch and thrush,
You're the best, right to the touch.

Ellen Watts (11)
Gomer Junior School

Movies

Some of these are very weepy,
When I watch the boring ones it makes me sleepy!

Some include me having to scream
Or even give me a very bad dream!

Some can make a very good story,
But on the other hand, some can be quite gory!

Some of them can be re-made,
But when they are the excitement will fade.

At last you're on the final scene
And you've spent hours looking at the screen!

If watching films is your favourite thing, you probably have bad eyes,
But I think I must admit, some films I do despise!

Joe Bavister (10)
Gomer Junior School

Music And Dance

You lull me to sleep on ribbons of sound,
Your voice so sweet and clear,
I can't tell you're here.
Shining waves ripple through my body,
All graceful and strong.

Rhythms I tap and rhythms I dance,
I try not to stop but you give me one glance.
I love to prance with every new dance.

I hear you whisper and I hear you loud,
But you always, always seem so very proud.
Oh please keep flowing, flowing to me.

Natalie Neal (11)
Gomer Junior School

Anger Within

A s a Spartan army you're hard to fight back
N ever-ending curses make me cause danger
G rowing hate and sadness inside
E verlasting walk from Heaven to Hell,
    consume and controls me under your spell,
    freezing my brain and stopping me to think,
R eleasing all the anger without a thought or blink.

W ithering anger and disgust for others
 I nside you blame your sister or brother
T hinking of the people who caused you the pain
H ating everyone, night and day
 I nsane thoughts which make you feel mad
N ot knowing the reason why you feel sad.

Nathan Sitch (10)
Gomer Junior School

Lady Macbeth

L osing her mind and sight slowly
A live with the excitement of murder
D aggers showing in her distressed mind
Y oung as she is, she has courage to kill the king

M aking her husband feel the guilt
A nger wound inside her
C ackles as the evilness in her heart grows
B lowing up her mind, she surprises herself
E nding the king's life was her downfall
'T is done
H ow can she act so innocent?

Elin Bebbington (10)
Gomer Junior School

Flowers

Your soft, gentle touch fills me with joy,
Your elegant figure sways in the meadow
Of red, white and blue.
Your broad smiling face lights up the night's sky
And smells so blissful and fresh.
Your tall slender legs standing so limp,
Yet delicate and strong.
Your sweet pastel colours
Make me lose my beauty,
For you are the prettiest of all!

Olivia Webb (11)
Gomer Junior School

Time

You're as swift as a snake
But cannot be caught,
Only a fool will try to catch you.

Since the beginning, you cannot be seen,
Your age is young but not known.
You can change yourself,
But people cannot change you.

Killing us slowly like a slow assassin
With invisible knives in your hands.

Jonathan Eaton (11)
Gomer Junior School

Music

M y body moves to your fascinating rhythm,
U ndescribable feelings prance in my mind.
S till I listen to your never-ending beating.
I n my body my heart thumps faster,
C aptivating rhythm that shakes my body and my feet.

Alice Cowan (10)
Gomer Junior School

The Monster

You rage in the deep, dark forest,
Waiting for prey to come.
The claws on your hands are so sharp,
They can rip through anything.
Your eyes twinkle like diamonds
In the dark, gloomy night.
Your footprints are so large
They could have humans living in them.
The roar from your mouth
Deafens us all.

You will eat anything
That gets in your way here and there.
The mysterious nature of you
Staggers all of us.
Who are you?

Rowan Pierce (11)
Gomer Junior School

Balloon

I see you following me,
Why?
Up there in the corner of my room,
Swaying like a ghost.
Why?
Pushing vases and pictures over,
You make me feel trapped and locked up.
Why?

I begin to feel safer as I watch you die.
Now you have become just
A shiny paper bag tied to a ribbon.
I am not scared at night anymore,
All you can do now is lie still on the floor.

Emma Newman (10)
Gomer Junior School

Fear

I'm scared of you,
Stop creeping up at me
From time to time,
I don't like you.
Your long, rough legs always touching me,
You freak me out.
Don't you get it?

You're so quiet
So I don't hear you.
Why tiptoe towards me
Then touch me in fright?

Sommer Rawlinson (11)
Gomer Junior School

The Magic Box

(Based on 'Magic Box' by Kit Wright)

I will put in my box . . .
An elegant, emotional elephant
Gliding through the air,
The smartest snake around town
And a big grizzly bear.

I will put in my box . . .
A whirling pool from an enchanted well,
A frosted diamond that's just vanished,
The multicoloured shell that's never been touched.

I will put in my box . . .
The first autumn leaf that's dropped off a tree,
A dash of light from the sun
And a familiar face on a puffy cloud.

My box is fashioned with golden sparks,
Glimmering from the stars above.

Emma Higham (10)
Heatherside Junior School

My Magic Box

(Based on 'Magic Box' by Kit Wright)

I will put in my box . . .
The last cry of a dying man,
The glistening glint of an evil eye,
A drop of blood dripping in a cave.

I will put in my box . . .
A sparkling diamond, namely the moon,
A silver swish of swans' feathers,
An effervescent lady with a grieving man.

I will put in my box . . .
A drop of midnight sparkling on the sea,
A scarlet emerald in a wintry wind,
The hot tears of a dying tiger.

I will put in my box . . .
The eerie whisper of steel on ice,
A misty grin, far from nice,
A dastardly bear burning bright!

I will put in my box . . .
A daring demon dancing on ice,
Death's door - when slamming shut,
The startled miaow of a puzzled mutt.

My box is made of ancient snow,
With death in the lock and life in the corners.
The hinges are monkey tails,
Still swinging in the trees.

There are demons in my box, angels too.
When it is open, the world turns to ice,
For my box is a box of dreams.

Alice Pooley (10)
Heatherside Junior School

The Magic Box

(Based on 'Magic Box' by Kit Wright)

I will put in my box . . .
The silk spiderwebs sparkling in the sun,
The ferocious, fire-fearing foreigners,
The roaring riot raging in Russia.

I will put in my box . . .
A game that can't be played,
A golden night shimmering,
A door that can't be opened.

I will put in my box . . .
The first words of my mouth,
My first tooth, as white as paper,
The desert sands of Cyprus, never stopping.

I will put in my box . . .
A whip that is used for massage,
A bench that you can't sit on,
A blue moon.

My box is fashioned from silver and
Lightning streaking through.
Emeralds are studded on its sides.
There are rocks from dead planets
Creating patterns on the lid, and
The corners have had meteors hit them.

I shall fly in my box,
Gliding through the solar system,
Then land on Pluto
And watch the planets cover the sun.

Padraíg Manning (9)
Heatherside Junior School

Magic Box

(Based on 'Magic Box' by Kit Wright)

I will put in my box . . .
A brutal boar with brittle tusks,
A seal all alone,
A rocky mountain with a slope going straight.

I will put in my box . . .
A vegetarian polar bear,
A tornado from China,
A sting from a manta ray.

I will put in my box . . .
Cattle from Jersey,
A lamb being born,
A fluffy bunny.

I will put in my box . . .
Spider-Man playing dolls,
A parrot ordering pizza,
A chicken going *quack.*

My box is
As light as a feather,
As quiet as an oak tree,
As beautiful as the sun.

I will share with my box
Irresistible knowledge,
The west wind blowing,
And friendship.

Emmie Mynott (10)
Heatherside Junior School

I Will Put In My Box . . .

(Based on 'Magic Box' by Kit Wright)

I will put in my box . . .
The sound of the sun soaring away,
The opening of a plane to endless paradise,
The stumble of a child's first walk.

I will put in my box . . .
The lightning strike from an angry god,
The touch of Australian dust,
The laugh of a hyena.

I will put in my box . . .
The last rock from Mount Everest,
The first miaow of a newborn kitten,
The last bark from a dog.

My box is fashioned with oak and swirls of gold,
Rubies as hinges.

I dream in my box
Of the birds singing
And water swirling,
Of dolphins leaping to and fro.

Alice Proctor (9)
Heatherside Junior School

Magic Box

(Based on 'Magic Box' by Kit Wright)

My box is fashioned
From silver metal
With a flower lid.

I will put in my box . . .
Cornwall with an indoor pool
Like bubblewrap.

I will put in my box . . .
Somerset with a playground outside,
Hopscotch, swings
And a sandpit with camping grass -
Sun shining down on us.

I will put in my box . . .
Five seasons and the golden moon,
A black cat in the house hole,
And a white mouse in a tree.

I will put in my box . . .
A rocket to fly to the moon so bright,
Do somersaults, backwards and forwards,
Floating around and around in space.

Emily Barden (9)
Heatherside Junior School

Magic Box

(Based on 'Magic Box' by Kit Wright)

I will put in my box . . .
A light shining off Lake Garda,
A wild horse munching happily,
A ladybird flying freely.

I will put in my box . . .
A favourite poem,
A snowman with a rumbling belly,
A story about people getting their rights.

I will put in my box . . .
The last look of a tired man,
The first mew of a kitten,
A joke written in Italian.

I will put in my box . . .
A fifth season, a blue moon,
A horse in a carriage,
A person pulling it.

My box is carved with animals
And made of wood painted lots of different colours.
The lid is sprinkled with moon dust.

I shall play netball in my box
On the hard ground,
Then run home with a trophy
The colour of the sun.

Zoe Styles (10)
Heatherside Junior School

My Box

(Based on 'Magic Box' by Kit Wright)

I will put in my box . . .
The stripes of a tiger,
A ball of nothingness from the depths of nowhere,
A splinter of turquoise sky.

I will put in my box . . .
A dewdrop from a spider's web,
A burning tip of a delicate flame,
A shadow captured in a mirror.

I will put in my box . . .
Whirling waters from where the world ends,
A fallen star whose light has gone out,
A streak of lightning stuck on a photograph.

My box is made from crepe paper,
The lock is made of a crab claw
And the hinges are caterpillars.

When you open the box,
Volcanoes in Hawaii erupt,
Avalanches fall in Iceland
And rainbows light up the lid.

I will dream in my box
About tigers and lightning
And flames in mirrors.

All in my box.

Amy Miller (10)
Heatherside Junior School

I Will Put In My Box . . .

(Based on 'Magic Box' by Kit Wright)

I will put in my box . . .
The sweet shine of a shooting star,
The clatter of flamenco dancers' castanets,
A dolphin diving deeply in the dark.

I will put in my box . . .
The breeze of a warm winter,
The dazzling sea shining softly,
A leaping spark of an electric fish.

I will put in my box . . .
Wild horses galloping freely,
The last cough of an uncle
And the first yelp of a puppy.

I will put in my box . . .
A fifth season and a dark sun,
A wolf in a red hood
And a girl with big fluffy ears.

My box is fashioned with lots of colours,
Yellow stars on the lid and secrets in the corners,
With a key of magic and horse hoof hinges.

I shall gallop in my box
Over the rocky mountainside
And see the multicoloured sunset.

Georgia Haldenby (9)
Heatherside Junior School

The Magic Box

(Based on 'Magic Box' by Kit Wright)

I will put in my box . . .
The silent sun stepping softly on the sea,
The west wind whistling quietly,
The moon moving magically around the misty sun.

I will put in my box . . .
A sunflower without a seed,
A Cyclops with three cat eyes,
An ear-piercing scream from a humpback whale.

I will put in my box . . .
A deadly illness that makes you better,
Glue that doesn't stick,
A stripy scarf that makes you cold.

My box is fashioned from gold and delicate feathers,
With galaxies in the corners and smiles from everyone.
Its hinges are the rays of the sun.

I shall fly in my box to the moon
On the finest snowflake ever made,
Then slowly float back to Earth
Where I belong.

Isabelle Davies (9)
Heatherside Junior School

Our Box

(Based on 'Magic Box' by Kit Wright)

I will put in our box . . .
The sweet song of a shooting star,
The joy of a screeching monkey,
The warmth of a new friend.

I will put in our box . . .
The blue water with a splash of grey sky,
The white sand of Mozambique,
And the warm sand of a storm.

I will put in our box . . .
Three precious moments,
The laugh of a baby
And the wrinkled smile
Of my much-loved gran.

I will put in our box . . .
A warm winter and a soft steel,
A hamster's yelp and a dog's squeal,
And a sparkle on a blunt mirror.

My box is made of a dragon's scales
And the breath of a tiger.
In the lock there is death,
But in the corner there is joy.
The hinges are made of a maiden's hair, soft and golden.

I shall freedive in my box
Down through the deep darkness and
Over the orange coral,
Then plummet to the sunlit sky.

Kemba Mitchell (10)
Heatherside Junior School

The Magic Box

(Based on 'Magic Box' by Kit Wright)

I will put in my box . . .
The pretty puff of a puffin,
The bouncy trot of a pony,
A spark of a firework.

I will put in my box . . .
A golden £8 note,
A grain of sand from Wales,
The tune of a songbird.

I will put in my box . . .
The shivering waves of you and me in the sea,
The first word a baby says,
The wobble of an old man.

I will shut in my box . . .
The winter's sun and the summer's snow,
A footballer in flippers
And a diver in shin pads.

My box is fashioned with hazel and icing sugar.
In the corners are nightmares and dreams.
The hinges are made from horseshoes.

I shall ride in my box
On the grounds of mud and horse dust,
Then get off the pony
With a smile as big as the sun.

Eve Boulter (10)
Heatherside Junior School

The Magic Box
(Based on 'Magic Box' by Kit Wright)

I will put in my box . . .
A summer's night playing in the street
And the warmth of the Cyprus sea.

I will put in my box . . .
The sound of an elephant's cry
And walking on the mountains of Wales.

I will put in my box . . .
A friend's last words
And the Golden Gates.

I will walk in my box
On the burning sun,
And only in my box.

My box is made from gold cloth
Sprinkled with frosted diamonds.
The lock decorated with silver stars,
Imported from space.
Ancient moon dust scattered along the lid.

Hayley Johnston (10)
Heatherside Junior School

Happiness

Happiness is yellow like the jolly, bright summer sun.
It sounds like birds tweeting on a summer's day,
It tastes like the most delicious ice cream you've ever tasted,
It smells like fresh air at the seaside,
It looks like the brightness of a new day coming up,
It feels like the warmth of the sun raising its wonderful rays,
It reminds me of summer with beautiful flowers and butterflies.

Anastasia Pybus (8)
John Keble CE Primary School

The Magic Box

(Based on 'Magic Box' by Kit Wright)

I will put in my box . . .
Five perfect summer pink magical wishes
Playing hide-and-seek.

I will put in my box . . .
Springy spring, fuzzy bunnies
Bouncing on the daisies.

I will put in my box . . .
Sparkling snowflakes floating gently down,
Making a thick, fluffy layer of snow.

It is fashioned from silver and gold
Shimmering stars in the pitch-black sky.

I will fly in my box over the
Magnificent Sydney Harbour Bridge
And over the astonishing Sydney Opera House.

I will put in my box . . .
Red, orange and brown autumn leaves
Floating elegantly to the ground.

Eryn Tyler-Smith (9)
John Keble CE Primary School

Love

Love is red like sweet poppies in a field,
It looks like bright red strawberries freshly picked,
It tastes like magnificent ripe watermelon,
It sounds like beautiful sweet singing birds in the countryside,
It smells like wild garlic in a shady wood,
It feels like a warming fire in your own home,
It reminds me of a garden full of red and yellow roses.

Georgia Lacey (8)
John Keble CE Primary School

The Magic Box

(Based on 'Magic Box' by Kit Wright)

I will put in my box . . .
The sweet smell of strawberry-flavoured ice cream,
The freezing cold ice from Antarctica,
The monstrous bloodthirsty monster from Mount Fiji.

I will put in my box . . .
The snow from the tip of Mount Everest,
The fever from the fierce fiery flying eagle,
The fine lock made from gold and silver.

I will put in my box . . .
20 missiles and 20 bombs
And roasting chocolate.

The box is fashioned from teeth,
From gold and silver it has lots of armour
And iron so other people can't get inside.

In my box I will visit Candy Land
And eat all the sweets and chocolate.

Oliver Piper (8)
John Keble CE Primary School

Happiness

Happiness is blue like a river,
It sounds like children playing happily,
It tastes like hot, sticky, chocolate cake,
It smells like hot Christmas pudding,
It looks like a beautiful rainbow,
It feels like my hand stroking a unicorn's back,
It reminds me of a world full of joyful people.

Jason Symons (8)
John Keble CE Primary School

The Magic Box
(Based on 'Magic Box' by Kit Wright)

I will put in my box . .
Twenty brilliant birthdays,
Sparkling in the sun, burning more every second.
An ancient pyramid and a huge Zurich ice rink.

I will put in my box . . .
A hundred raspberry love cakes,
The gingery, golden sunshine,
And one thousand buttery pancakes.

My box is fashioned from wood and rubies,
And steel with pictures of swimming pools on the lid
With secrets inside.
The hinges are made from an old iron ship.

I will sail in my box at Burfield Sailing Club
And I will land on the islands.
Then we will come to the shore,
The beach is the colour of the golden sunshine.

Jonathan Greene (8)
John Keble CE Primary School

Love

Love is red like a lovely rose in the summer.
Love sounds like beautiful flute music.
Love tastes like a sweet red cherry.
Love smells like a delightful rose.
Love looks like a tender, romantic dinner.
Love feels like a smooth rose petal.
Love reminds me of my mum and dad when they got married.

Amelia Victoria (8)
John Keble CE Primary School

The Magic Box

(Based on 'Magic Box' by Kit Wright)

I will put in the box . . .
A yellow flower just too pretty to pick
And an entertaining clown to make people laugh.

My box is fashioned from smooth wood
With a gold padlock.

It has wishes and goodness inside,
With a friendly old lady showing
Me the way to my gingerbread house,
That has candy sticks for trees
And a biscuit for a door.
It is so tempting to eat.

I would fly on a broomstick with the other good witches.
I hope the witches won't turn me into a frog.

Amy Joseph (9)
John Keble CE Primary School

The Magic Box

(Based on 'Magic Box' by Kit Wright)

I will put in my box . . .
A wooden bungee jumper made of snow
That never melts,
And a book that has no end.

I will put in my box . . .
A Pluto that is bigger than Jupiter,
And a fiery, multicoloured motorcycle.

It is fashioned from rubies and diamonds,
Emeralds and sparkling sapphires
On a summer night.

In my box I would win the lottery every week
And build a space hotel and a time machine.

Calvin Jarman (8)
John Keble CE Primary School

The Magic Box

(Based on 'Magic Box' by Kit Wright)

I will put in my box . . .
The sparkling snow from a frosty ledge,
Five enchanted spring wishes
And a flowing, floral, elegant dress.

I will put in my box . . .
A brand new flower with the scent of perfume,
A sniff of the newest dress,
And three secrets spoken in French.

My box is fashioned from smooth wood
With butterflies on the lid.
Its hinges are the sparkling icicles of the Arctic.

I shall skip happily through a meadow full of flowers
And end the day by having a slice of delicious cake.

Ellie Dickson (8)
John Keble CE Primary School

The Magic Box

(Based on 'Magic Box' by Kit Wright)

I will put in my box . . .
The massive Taj Mahal on a lollipop stick
With sweet, stylish strawberries and tasty toffee sauce!
Sweetie Land with all the sweets in the world
On a green ice cream cone with a flake. Yum-yum.

I will put in my box . . .
The powerful stab of a lightsaber,
The electric bolts of the Emperor,
The strangle of the Sith lord killing his enemy.

It is fashioned from Star Wars, lightsabers and blasters.
Its hinges are like the door of the Millennium Falcon.

In my box I will fight in battle,
And fight till they die.

George Rayner (8)
John Keble CE Primary School

Fun

Fun is orange like the big burning-hot sun blazing in the sky,
It sounds like sizzling sausages cooking fiercely on a barbecue,
It tastes like fresh, hot, baking, potato crisps,
It smells like steam from a red-hot sun in the sky,
It looks like children playing under a humungous chestnut tree,
It feels like a lovely fluffy blanket,
It reminds me of a roasting summer's day.

Cameron Thomson (7)
John Keble CE Primary School

Anger

Anger is like a red-hot fire,
It sounds like a lion roaring its head off,
It tastes like red-hot chillies,
It smells like smoke from a fierce forest fire,
It looks like a dangerous lion attacking a newborn calf,
It feels soft and melting like metal in a blast furnace,
It reminds me of stamping to my bedroom when Mummy tells me off.

Ethan Pell (8)
John Keble CE Primary School

Happiness

Happiness is yellow like a beautiful sunflower swaying in the breeze,
It sounds like young children running on fresh green grass,
It tastes like fresh lemonade cooling my body down,
It smells like fresh fruit in a fruit bowl,
It looks like rolling hills covered in poppies,
It feels like fairies dancing all around me.

Katie Williamson-Jones (8)
John Keble CE Primary School

Happiness

Happiness is pink like the roses in the summer,
It sounds like the wind whistling in the trees,
It tastes like strawberries and cream,
It smells like the sugar in the river in the park,
It looks like rabbits hopping in the sun,
It feels like fresh air in the sky,
It reminds me of the *world!*

Rosie Welch (7)
John Keble CE Primary School

Love

Love is pink like beautiful love hearts,
It sounds like a wonderful choir singing,
It smells like scented poppies in a meadow,
It tastes like lovely melted chocolate left in the sun,
It feels like a cute, warm, smooth cat,
It looks like lovely fireworks bursting into the air,
It reminds me of a beautiful sunset lowering into the sea.

Emma Harwood (9)
John Keble CE Primary School

Happiness

Happiness is the colour yellow.
Happiness makes me smile.
Happiness is when I go to the One Stop Shop.
Happiness is playing happy families.
Happiness makes me feel good.
Happiness is when I eat Aero Bubbles.

Jonathan Ling (8)
John Keble CE Primary School

Using My Senses

I enjoy seeing the bare horse chestnut tree
Waiting to grow its leaves again.

I can taste the warm fresh air entering my mouth
Like a soft pillow which I can lie on.

I do feel the hot sun tanning my cheeks
As if I am in a hot desert, making me sweat like a pool.

I love to watch the bird doing acrobatics in the air
And landing with perfect balance.

I like the smell of the summer fresh air
Wafting up my nostrils.

I listen to the screaming children shouting their heads off
Like a gorilla doing its loudest screech.

Mason Tyler-Smith (7)
John Keble CE Primary School

Using My Senses

I can hear the deafening flocks of pitch-black
blackbirds soaring silently through the sky.

I love feeling rough grey concrete of the playground
when I race up and down.

I can see the beautiful burning sun scorching high in
the beaming, bright blue brilliant sky.

I love watching little bluebirds
hopping on the grassy green field.

I can taste the cool breeze wildly blowing
in my watering mouth.

I love smelling the damp whiff of yellow wood
chippings scattered everywhere.

Frankie Taylor (9)
John Keble CE Primary School

Using My Senses

I can taste the fresh, ice-cold water
When I take a long drink
After I have been running in a race.

I can feel the rough stone playground
When I fall over and hurt a knee.

I can see the empty football pitch
That is covered in slippery mud.

I can watch the little children
Playing in the bright yellow sand.

I can hear the roaring lorries and cars
Zooming down the road.

I can smell the stinking, whiffing and ponging manure
That makes me suffocate.

Emily Baker (8)
John Keble CE Primary School

Using My Senses

I love to smell the lovely red roses
And the yellow daffodils swishing in the wind.

I like to watch the children playing with each other,
Like playing football and basketball.

I do love feeling the blazing sun
And hot air on my skin.

I can hear the engines of cars on the road,
And the noisy birds twittering on.

I enjoy tasting the cold, freezing my mouth
And freezing me to a statue.

Lula Dickson (7)
John Keble CE Primary School

Happiness

Happiness is the colour of yellow and a gleaming sun,
It sounds like birds singing on a tree and
Tastes like smelling chocolates melted in the sun.
It smells of amazing lavender,
It looks like a colourful sculpture made out of gold
And it feels very smooth and soft like a cushion,
And it reminds me of my friends.

Joe Arthur (8)
John Keble CE Primary School

Anger

Anger is hatred bubbling in your brain,
It sounds like someone being boiled alive,
It tastes like red-hot chillies burning on your tongue,
It smells like rotten eggs,
It looks like something cruel,
It feels like ghostly fingers touching you,
It reminds me of a very horrid time in my life.

Jehian Tiley (7)
John Keble CE Primary School

Love

Love is red like a beautiful love heart,
It sounds like colourful fireworks fizzing into the pink sky,
It tastes like delicious chocolates formed in hearts,
It smells like a scented rose,
It looks like a couple on the beach watching the sun go down,
It reminds me of my mum and dad getting married.

Lalie Carlod (9)
John Keble CE Primary School

Anger

Anger reminds me of the colour red, like my heartbeat.
Anger sounds like an earthquake rumbling from the other side
of the world.
Anger tastes like me and my friend having a fight.
Anger smells like a crumbling war.
Anger looks like someone hanging dead.
Anger feels like a slithery eyeball.
Anger reminds me of when my grandpa told me he got shot
in the hip.

Bea Golley (8)
John Keble CE Primary School

Anger

Anger is the colour red, like the destruction of an earthquake,
It sounds like a blazing fire burning a town,
It tastes like a chainsaw cutting your mouth open,
It smells like onions that make you cry,
It looks like a tiger killing its prey,
It feels like a lion scouring the jungle,
It reminds me of a beating drum getting louder and faster.

Charles Hurst (7)
John Keble CE Primary School

Fear

It sounds like a fierce hunting wolf,
It tastes like a sour toxic waste,
It smells like beautiful roses,
It feels like a bumpy, massive rock.

Ellie Mackinnon (9)
John Keble CE Primary School

What Makes Me Happy

Happiness is pink like the sky up above.
Happiness reminds me of a white dove swooping in the air,
Happiness tastes like whipped cream and cherries,
Happiness looks like a group of close friends,
Happiness sounds like chirping of bluebirds in a blossom tree,
Happiness feels like a pink fluffy pillow that everyone loves,
Happiness smells like roses that are new to the world.

Shannon Allen (10)
Knights Enham Junior School

Fear

Fear is as dark as a midnight sky.
Fear feels like a tingle down your back.
Fear sounds like a quiet whisper in the air.
Fear reminds me of a dark winter's night.
Fear smells like a strong clove of garlic.
It tastes like salt sliding down your throat.
It looks like red eyes in the distance.

Chelsee James (10)
Knights Enham Junior School

My Feelings

My emotions flood over me like a blue ocean wave lapping on a beach.
I'm always cheerful when the bright yellow sun comes out.
Tiredness is when I fall into a deep dark blue sleep.
My heart is as red as a rose.

Deanne Johnson-May (10)
Knights Enham Junior School

Passion For Love

Love tastes like a gorgeous box of chocolates.
Love looks like a bunch of freshly picked roses.
It feels like a new, red, soft, fluffy cushion full of red feathers.
It sounds like a new CD player playing quiet jazz in the background.
Love smells like freshly made sweets just packed a few minutes ago.
It reminds me of cut-out hearts following me through the fields.

Do you have a passion for love?

Maya Loaiza (9)
Knights Enham Junior School

Fear Is Black

Fear is black like a dead day,
Fear looks like a black hole that spreads all over the world,
Fear tastes like dead rats on a stick,
Fear smells like smoky burnt toast,
Fear reminds me of death,
Fear sounds like a shrieking bat,
Fear feels like a lonely grave.

Sky Charmaine Taylor (9)
Knights Enham Junior School

My Love

L ove is red like my beating heart,
O ften helping me sleep through the dark.
V ery red, my heart goes *boom,*
E very time I feel love in my room.

Abi Buckland (9)
Knights Enham Junior School

The Sweet Scent Of Laughter

Laughter smells like the sweet, special scent of a beautiful spring
or summer's day,
It looks like beautiful, amazing animals,
It feels like happiness but it has a new, special twist,
It sounds like young, happy children spreading their happiness,
It looks like creamy mint chocolate chip ice cream,
Laughter reminds me of the closeness I feel
when with the people I love.

Keeya Hanley (9)
Knights Enham Junior School

Love

Love reminds me of a cuddly teddy bear.
Love sounds like warming jazz in a romantic restaurant.
Love looks like the first red rose.
Love feels like running through green, green grass.
Love smells like melted chocs.
Love tastes like sweet, sweet honey.

Deanna Archer (10)
Knights Enham Junior School

Anger Is Hot

Anger is red like a bubbly volcano,
as hot as curry freshly made.
It feels like bacon spitting in your face,
like tripping over your shoelace.
It's like hot water exploding in your face,
a burnt chicken, nothing to taste.

Matthew Blake (9)
Knights Enham Junior School

Anger

Anger is red like boiling blood.
Anger is a rocket waiting to burst.
Anger is a taste of a burnt sizzled sausage.
Anger sounds like a ticking bomb.
Anger reminds me of a zooming car.
Anger feels like a massive explosion.
Anger smells like hot lava.

Connor Durbridge (9)
Knights Enham Junior School

Love

Love is as gentle as a dove,
When you're feeling it, romantic love songs rush through your head.
You are dreaming about it all the time you are in bed.
Love feels like a warm hug that's lovely and snug.
Love smells like freshly picked roses.
Love is pink like spring blossom.

Jade Goddard (9)
Knights Enham Junior School

Laughter Is Fun

It smells like the sweet scent of a beautiful pink rose.
It feels like a kiss of love.
It reminds me of a lovely summer's day.
It sounds like an happy angel calling.
Laughter tastes like happiness with a twist.
Laughter looks like a very special friendship growing.

Abbie Jessica Haswell (10)
Knights Enham Junior School

My Magic Box

(Based on 'Magic Box' by Kit Wright)

I will put in my box . . .

A hot tub under the silky summer sky,
A warm, snugly bed,
A comfy couch with cosy cushions.

I will put in my box . . .

A huge green football pitch,
A glamorous, groovy games room,
A smooth, exciting race track.

I will put in my box . . .

A treasure chest full of shining glory,
A posh modern house,
A healthy life and rich living.

I will put in my box . . .

A wonderland in a snowy place,
A fiery sun above Dreamland,
The wonderful, grateful Earth.

Kurtis Archer (11)
Knights Enham Junior School

Happiness

Happiness looks like a beautiful summer's morning.
Happiness feels like a warm fluffy pillow.
Happiness smells like creamy chocolate.
Happiness reminds me of a hot day.
Happiness tastes like strawberry cream.
Happiness sounds like love.

Bruce Shaw (10)
Knights Enham Junior School

My Magic Box

(Based on 'Magic Box' by Kit Wright)

In my magic box . . .
Monsters sweep the skies.
In my magic box . . .
Witches fly up high.

In my magic box . . .
Magicians pull bunnies from hats.
In my magic box . . .
Wizards fly on mats.

In my magic box . . .
Skies are black.
In my magic box . . .
We live with killer cats.

In my magic box . . .
Pictures move.
In my magic box . . .
Dragons groove.

Billy Duffy (11)
Knights Enham Junior School

The Reason Of Anger

Anger is red like a London bus,
Red like fire,
Red like blood,
Red like your heart,
Red like a red box,
Red like red hair,
Red like a red tray.   ·

Tom Lant (9)
Knights Enham Junior School

Love Is In The Air

Love smells like a bunch of bright red roses just picked.
Love feels warm and cosy like a hot chocolate
with a blazing fire burning.
Love tastes like yummy ice cream melting on your tongue
with millions of chocolate sprinkles for an extra touch.
Love reminds me of a beautiful summer's day when I'm running
through the fields of grass and beautiful bright red roses.
Love looks like a romantic double king-sized bed
with loads of chocs in a beautiful box for you to eat today.

Kirsten Armstrong (10)
Knights Enham Junior School

Laughter

Laugher smells like an incredibly beautiful sunset,
Laughter feels like a heart-warming hug,
Laughter sounds like baby birds singing,
Laughter tastes like cream and buns,
Laughter looks like a heart of joy,
Laugher reminds me of the person inside . . .
                                        me!

Kaitlin Fairchild (10)
Knights Enham Junior School

My Feelings

My tiredness came over me like my white duvet.
My happiness was as yellow as the sun shining through my windows.
My kindness was as pink as my sister's spoon as I fed her,
                                        her breakfast.
My cheerfulness made everyone around me happy.

Laura Hanson (9)
Knights Enham Junior School

Anger Madness

Anger is red like a boiling volcano.
Anger reminds me of a raging hot fire.
Anger tastes like a sizzling sausage as hot as the sun.
Anger looks as disturbed as a Tyrannosaurus-rex.
Anger sounds like the peep-peep of a train.
Anger smells like a rotten fish.
Anger feels like a crisp going down your throat sideways.

Callum Paxton (10)
Knights Enham Junior School

Chelsea

C heerfully I shout when Chelsea score
H appily I jump around when they score
E xcitement, everyone is singing
L aughter is heard all around
S uccess, we win!
E veryone stands when Chelsea scores
A t the end I will always love Chelsea.

Gemma Blake (9)
Knights Enham Junior School

Chloe's Emotions

My love is like a red love heart on Valentine's Day.
My happiness is like the orange sand on the beach.
My pain is like a tear falling from the sky.
My anger is like a red fire engine.

　　　My emotions make me!

Chloe Gleed (9)
Knights Enham Junior School

My Magic Box
(Based on 'Magic Box' by Kit Wright)

I will put in my box . . .
Some silky sand that once lay on the beach of a magical land.
A small dwarf selling shiny golden coins stolen from the north.
A gleaming fin off a small, shy, sleeping dolphin.

I will also put in my box . . .
A whiff of sweet scent carried gracefully by the wind.
A historical artefact with ancient shapes.
The current of the wide Mediterranean.

I will put in my box . . .
The first hug for a newborn baby.
One scarlet wish from a child desperate for peace.
The last breath of a departed loved one.

My box is fashioned from the finest silver with a snow-covered inside.
It has stars all over and new worlds in each corner.
Its hinges are the locks on a diary.

I will learn in my box about all the dangers and needs of the world,
Then play with the magic with friends and family
And have all the love that I need.

Katie Dutton (10)
Knights Enham Junior School

My Feelings

Love is like the reddest rose growing around me.
Anger is like a fire when I have a barbecue.
Tiredness is like me in space falling past stars.
Happiness is like the sun bursting through the clouds when I smile.
Sadness is like the rain when I cry and tears run down my face.
Cheerfulness is like the rainbow and its colour
                              when I'm dancing around.
Illness is like the wind blowing when I cough.

Jessica Hall (9)
Knights Enham Junior School

I Will Put In My Box . . .
(Based on 'Magic Box' by Kit Wright)

I will put in my box . . .
The first football ever made on Earth,
A rock of lava from the ancient Mount Yellowstones,
The cleanest bowl of water from the River Mississippi.

I will put in my box . . .
A rabbit racing a resentful racoon,
Fire from the mouth of an enormous dragon,
Ten wishes from a genie with great power.

I will put in my box . . .
A dangerous dinosaur from prehistoric times,
A red spotty alien from Pluto,
A chocolate waterfall in a tropical jungle.

I will put in my box . . .
A golden piece of treasure from an Egyptian pyramid,
Bronze, silver and gold coins, all shapes and sizes,
Secret codes to unlock or find magical treasure.

My box is cool and covered in decorated footballs, all different sizes.
The corners are full of special sports records.
The sides are like walls holding secrets inside.

I shall keep my box until my heart stops beating
And then I shall open the box and set them all free.

Brendan Harris (10)
Knights Enham Junior School

Anger Is Red

Anger is red like an explosion of lava,
It reminds me of boiling hot water,
It feels like jumping into a thorn bush,
It tastes like red-hot chilli peppers,
It smells like a mouldy rotten egg,
It sounds like a tumbling wall,
It looks like an angry bull.

Matthew Lovering (10)
Knights Enham Junior School

My Magic Box

(Based on 'Magic Box' by Kit Wright)

In my magic box . . .
There is a bouncing banana beating a bear.

In my magic box . . .
There is a fat footballer chasing a ferret.

In my magic box . . .
There is a wicked witch whistling wildly.

Jack Tough (10)
Knights Enham Junior School

Anger

Anger looks like a dragon's flaming fire,
Anger is like lava exploding from volcanoes,
Anger feels like you're going to burst with bright flames coming out
                                                    of your head,
Anger tastes like your heart on a spike,
Anger reminds me of exploding planes in the sky.

Frankie Horton (9)
Knights Enham Junior School

Nicole's Emotions

Love is like a red heart in the sky.
Love is like a red heart in your body.
Love is red like blood running from a leg.

Happiness is like sand on a sunny beach.
Happiness is like a sunny day at the park.

Nicole Underhill (9)
Knights Enham Junior School

My Magic Box

(Based on 'Magic Box' by Kit Wright)

I will put in my box . . .
The memories of many loved ones
The smell of fresh apple pie in the morning.

I will put in my box . . .
The power of the rough sea
The sound of a laughing baby.

I will put in my box . . .
A dog made of chocolate monsters
A cat made of tuna fish.

I will put in my box . . .
Fairy dust that really is gold
Pink grass and green carnations.

My box is made of an old shoe box decorated with flowers, stars
and dolphins.
My box is full of mystery.

I will keep my hopes and dreams in my box.
With my box I will travel and explore the wonderful world.

Katie Turner (10)
Knights Enham Junior School

Happiness

H elpfulness is when you help someone.
A nger is when your face goes red.
P ain is when you have hurt yourself.
P eaceful
 I s when you have no noise.
N ice is when you are nice.
E xcitement is like Chelsea winning their football matches.
S adness is when you have a broken heart.
S urprised is when you know you have something new.

Jade Trowbridge (9)
Knights Enham Junior School

My Magic Box
(Based on 'Magic Box' by Kit Wright)

I will put in my box . . .
All of my frocks
And sometimes it's where I keep my odd socks.

I will put in my box . . .
Lots of red streams
And floaty dreams made of candyfloss.

I will put in my box . . .
Purple shells covered in lovely smells.

I will put in my box . . .
Snowflakes on pancakes.

I will put in my box . . .
Flying bunnies and bouncing birds.

On my box there is rainbow dust.
On the sides and in the corners there is snow.
On the lid there is a glass butterfly.

Charlie Sweet (11)
Knights Enham Junior School

My Magic Box
(Based on 'Magic Box' by Kit Wright)

In my magic box I'll put . . .
Friends and foes in the corners.

In my magic box I'll put . . .
Happiness and smiles.

In my magic box I'll put . . .
Pizza and crisps.

In my magic box I'll put . . .
Cuddles and love.

Dominic Howitt (11)
Knights Enham Junior School

Love

Love is pink like a beautiful rose.
Love is so great it tickles my nose.
Love sounds like birds singing in a tree.
Love just makes me so, so, so happy.
Love tastes like strawberries with a whip of cream.
Someone who loves you will never be mean.
Love reminds me of a big bunch of happiness.
If someone loves you, they will give you a kiss.
Love smells like freedom coming from the heart.
If you love someone dearly you'll never be apart.
Love feels like someone being there for you.
If you love me, I love you too!

Carma Newell (10)
Knights Enham Junior School

In My Magic Box

(Based on 'Magic Box' by Kit Wright)

In my magic box I will put . . .
A paper flower decorated with grey and white petals.

In my magic box I will put . . .
A big grey butterfly with a baby.

In my magic box I will put . . .
A grey and white hairband.

In my magic box I will put . . .
A pair of clean white socks.

My magic box is fashioned with red glitter and silver plants.

Shannon Maxim (10)
Knights Enham Junior School

Miss Howard's Head

A teacher's head such as Miss Howard's is so full of ideas
In fact you can't fit the brain itself
So bulging and violent
They fly into her ear then swim out of the mouth
The words and the learning gas itself
And fly silently
So softly and sweetly with great feat
So watch out, Miss Howard is about
Miss Howard
Miss Howard!
Miss Howard . . . look out!

Ben Ireland (11)
Milton Park Junior School

My Poem

I have a cupboard on the back of my head
The keyhole is rusty
So I get some WD40, so I can open it
It opens . . . all the ideas come to me
I am amazed, I am flying through my work
I am done and then something happens
All my ideas go, I am sad
Bye-bye cupboard, bye-bye ideas
Now my brain is lonely.

Brandon Shaw (10)
Milton Park Junior School

A Boy's Head

A boy's head is full of schoolchildren larking about,
Warplanes ready to battle homework diaries and hard sums,
Tourists coming from far and wide,
Departing and arriving in different parts of a vast imagination.

Alexander Whitcomb (10)
Milton Park Junior School

Things I Like

I like my friends, they're really fun,
I also like playing in the sun.
Playing in the pool is very nice,
but it's as cold as ice.
I like going to the beach, in the sea,
waiting for the ball to be passed to me.
I love rabbits, they mean the world to me
with their bushy tails, and they're so friendly.
It's fab going away on holiday,
doing different stuff every day.
I love penguins, they're so cool,
they like to go for a dip in the pool.
Shopping is the best fun,
new stuff for everyone.

Adrienne Godden (10)
Oakfield Primary School

Can I Go To The Park Today?

'Can I go to the park today?'
My mum said, 'No way!'
'Can I go to the park today?'
My mum said, 'Go away!'
I stomped up to my room,
Made quite a lot of mess,
'Can I go to the park today?'
My mum was pretty stressed,
So she turned round and said, 'Yes!'

Dee-Cha Henderson (9)
Oakfield Primary School

Things I Like

I have two dogs that I love so much,
They are very cute and soft to touch.
I feed them and groom them, which I think is cool,
They love it so much that they give me their paw.

I love toys, especially if they're soft,
I have loads on my bed and thousands in the loft.
Roxy's my favourite, she has her own clothes,
She has a white face with a brown nose.

I love trampolining, I bounce very high,
It feels like I can touch the sky.
I love to swim I think it's so fun,
I go once a week and take along my mum.

But best of all, I love annoying my dad,
I sit and jump on him which makes him mad.
Then he tickles me and makes me laugh,
Then he chases me up the garden path.

As you can see, these are my favourite things I like,
Oh, one more thing, I love riding my bike!

Laura Brooks (10)
Oakfield Primary School

I Wish . . .

I wish I were a football player
Scoring loads of goals.
I wish I supported Liverpool
Wearing red and red shorts.
I wish I were called Fernando Torres.
I wish I had a Bugatti Veyron.
And I wish I had a million pounds
And made food for myself.
I wish my cake would never run out.

Lars Meidell (8)
St Winifred's School, Southampton

Haunted House

On the top of the hill sits a massive house.
Black shabby walls, black roof, cracked windows.
Meat with flies on it,
Knives with blood on them.
Owls eating rats on the creaking floors,
Owls tu-whit, tu-whooing all night long,
Cooing at the break of dawn,
Flying around the roofs,
Owls sitting on graves.
Rats running up and down the stairs,
Scuttling under the floorboards.
Creaky chairs sitting under tables,
Broken lights flickering in the darkness.
Air smelling of bones in soil,
Ghosts knocking on doors.
Ghosts in the darkness.

George Parrott (8)
St Winifred's School, Southampton

The Attic

Up in the attic many say
'What's this?'
'Where's that from?'
'How did that get there?'
Bit and bobs from way back when,
Knick-knacks from there and then,
Bric-a-brac and souvenirs collected for who knows why,
Old, ancient, dusty junk kept to hold onto the past,
Memories stored in big brown boxes, bags, books and photo albums,
Pictures and pictures from, oh, I don't know when!
Old gas masks and rocking horses, all part of history before now.
The attic, reminders of happy, bad or even sad times
But still a magical place!

Georgia Parker (11)
St Winifred's School, Southampton

Favourite Food

There are all kinds of food,
Crunchy food, juicy food and soft food.
Take meatballs, for example,
My favourite food, covered in rich tomato sauce.
Pasta, oh pasta!
Where do I begin?
Red pasta, yellow pasta and green pasta,
All smothered in butter.
What next? I wonder,
Roasted, boiled or stewed?
What can this be?
What a surprise,
It's the chicken.
Next to pasta and meatballs,
It's my favourite food.
Well, that's it,
My favourite foods,
Where would I be without them?

Adam Johnston (11)
St Winifred's School, Southampton

My Puppy

My puppy, white with brown spots,
A small springer spaniel.
Rosie's her name.
She loves treats, food,
Going outside, squeaky teddies and toys.
As cuddly as the softest teddy,
So soft you could go to sleep with her.
She hates having a bath,
And is very mucky all the time.
She follows me as if to say
'I love you!'

Emily Lewis (11)
St Winifred's School, Southampton

The Alien

Ten golden eyes like a football,
Red slimy skin.
Two gloopy mouths.
A thousand yellow claws.
Bright orange hair.
Fifteen hundred black legs.
His spaceship has
Large windows,
Triangular doors,
Red levers,
Black guns,
Yellow buttons . . .

He flies off home.

Samuel Riley (9)
St Winifred's School, Southampton

I Wish . . .

I wish my name were Don
I wish I had a cool car
Then I wish I were a Roman
Going to war fighting the Celts

I wish I were a wizard
Saying loads of spells
I wish I were a spy
Spying on what people were doing

I wish I were an Anglo Saxon
Fighting the Vikings
Firing arrows.

Sanjiv Gill (8)
St Winifred's School, Southampton

I Wish . . .

I wish I were a transformer to crush everything in my path
And kill every enemy.
I would transform into a machine.

And I wish I were a big bug to eat everyone.
I wish I were a skilled football player
Scoring goals.

I wish I could fly as high as a spaceship.
I wish I could ride a skateboard like the big boys.

Jeevan Sahota (7)
St Winifred's School, Southampton

Clocks

Early alarm bell wakes me up!
I hate the tick, tick, ticking.
It's ticking as noisily as a giant metronome.
I slam my hand on the button
And it falls to the floor with a bang!

Some clocks' bells ring on the hour, or half-past,
But my clock's bell rings every ten minutes!
Clocks are annoying, *tick-tock! Ding! Ding!*

Stephen Whorwood (10)
St Winifred's School, Southampton

Movies

Movies, funny clowns slipping on banana peel.
Scary Grim Reaper taking souls to the land of the dead.
FBI cops chasing thieves and gangs.
Fantasy elves pursuing evil overlords.
Superheroes shooting spiderwebs, looking through walls,
Bending metal with their super strength.

Tristan Harley (11)
St Winifred's School, Southampton

Food

Pancakes piled up on a plate,
Pink pasta platter,
Pepperoni and pork pizza,
Cravings for crunchy cod,
Contentment with cool chocolate,
Big and bland veggie burgers,
Peeled bananas, smelling sweet and alluring,
Grilled hoki steaming hot,
Mexican chilli, spicy and nice.

Joseph Seymour (10)
St Winifred's School, Southampton

I Wish . . .

I wish I could fly so I could see
All different countries.
I wish I had £999 999 999
That would never run out
So that I could buy everything I wanted
Like the fastest jet car ever.
I wish you did not have to take injections and tablets.
I wish the world were made out of sweets and chocolate.

George Vincent (8)
St Winifred's School, Southampton

South Air Train

Buffet car full of sounds,
Crisps as crunchy as dropping stones,
Coffee as safe as a volcano's lava.
Fizzy drinks, as fizzy as lemonade,
The body, fat as Poland.
All the stations are international.
This is the South Air Train.

Simon Solecki (8)
St Winifred's School, Southampton

The Sea

The sea is the king of the land,
The sea wears the crown of coral,
With whales as children,
And eels as scarves.

The sea has dolphins as friends,
The fish are the sea's shoes,
For the sea has pearls as jewels,
The sea's clothes are plants.

Tropical fish swimming through the reef,
A sparkling rainbow glimmering in the sun.
Pufferfish, clownfish, angelfish and lion fish;
Colourful clownfish counting eggs.
Pufferfish panic-stricken puffing themselves up,
Angelfish annoying their friends with their perfect ways,
Lion fish stalking their prey.

Alice Borodzicz (10)
St Winifred's School, Southampton

I Wish . . .

I wish I were a scientist
Who built a laser
To blow up school
(I'd evacuate it first)
And I had all the boy books in the world
And read them all
I wish the world were made of books
I wish I were a mechanic
Who fixed the biggest lorry in the world
I wish I built a Lego world.

Kieran Harrison (7)
St Winifred's School, Southampton

I Wish . . .

I wish I were driving a Ferrari with the speed monitor on 1,000!
I wish I could stay up all night driving at 1,000mph.
I wish I were driving a Pendolino.
I wish I could fly with the RAF and go up and up and up
And I wish I were *cool!*
I wish I had more than two hundred bottles of Coke,
Make that two thousand bottles of Coke.
I wish I could have ten birthdays a year.

Victor Smith (8)
St Winifred's School, Southampton

The Moon

I'm the shimmering, shining, silver queen of the night.
Glowing, glittering, gleaming, gliding across the sky.
I pull the waves up on your shores.
Flashing my bright eyes, I give you light in your hours of darkness.
I sing my silent song to the stunning stars of the night.
Then I look across the sky to say hello
To my beaming, blistering mother, the sun.
But, with a crash, night turns to day and I sleep till the stars
                                                    shine again.

Alice Denham (10)
St Winifred's School, Southampton

I Wish . . .

I wish I had a pet lion called Nick,
With fur as gold as the gleaming sun.
As deadly as a poison sting,
Cunning as a fox,
Strong as a bear
And quick as a hare.

Samuel Johnson
St Winifred's School, Southampton

The Night-Light Mouse

I was working in the lab late one night,
I opened my desk and received a fright.
There sat a mouse, eating some cheese,
He didn't say thank you, he didn't say please.
He didn't say hi, hello or goodbye,
He just nibbled the cheese with a gleam in his eye.
I saw that the mouse gave a source of light,
In horror I realised his awful plight.
He'd drunk all my potion,
Oh, what an emotion!
In the end I used him
As a nice night-light.
That sorted out the mouse all right!

Francesca Mylod-Ford (9)
St Winifred's School, Southampton

Chocolate

Peel off the silver wrapper,
Snap the crunchy chocolate in half
And eat it all!
It's so good,
It tastes like gold.

Brown, white and dark,
It's so creamy, delicious,
Munchy and scrumptious.

I will just eat it all in one bite . . .
Yummy!

Stephen Follows (9)
St Winifred's School, Southampton

Aliens

Skin, rough, slimy and white
Eight massive eyes, shining like eight red suns
Nose, thin with twenty nostrils as big as an elephant's
It has a million arms like a centipede's legs
As ugly as a troll
Its head, as big as the moon
Squidgy fat covering his wobbly body
He is as heavy as a jumbo jet
He goes around eating people
Sliming along the ground like a giant slug.

Max McHugh (9)
St Winifred's School, Southampton

I Wish . . .

I wish it were time for tea
And my mum had put a bowl in front of me
And in the bowl I could see
There was a boat in front of me
Bobbing up and down on a sea
Made of jelly
And beside the boat I would see
Two fish and all I would hear would be
Blub, blub, blub!

Orla McGinnis (8)
St Winifred's School, Southampton

Deborah - Cinquain

Deborah,
Funny, cheeky,
She is great at dancing,
Absolutely loves Playmobil,
My friend.

Flora Burleigh (11)
Steep CE Primary School

Sisters - Cinquain

Sisters.
Full on crazy.
They are quite annoying.
They are also so very nice.
Sisters.

Joshua Rolison (10)
Steep CE Primary School

Homework - Cinquain

Homework
Boring and hard.
You have to do at home.
It makes me mad when I do it.
Stressful.

Amy Jo Holden (9)
Steep CE Primary School

Young Bond - Cinquain

Young Bond
Magnificent
House jumper, roof leaper,
Scared but confident and quite sad
Bravest!

Dominic Young-Ballinger (9)
Steep CE Primary School

Sweeties - Cinquain

Sweeties
Sweeties are great
All fizzy in your mouth
Bonbons land in your big mouth
Yum-yum.

Reuben Harry (9)
Steep CE Primary School

Friday - Cinquain

Friday
Near the weekend
Running, shouting, 'Friday!
Thank God, it's Friday, I'm joyful
Hooray!'

Cameron Martin (11)
Steep CE Primary School

A Dove - Cinquain

A dove.
Solemn and soft.
Flying high in the sky.
I feel excited when it's near.
My bird.

Evelyn Kay Blackwell (9)
Steep CE Primary School

Reading - Cinquain

Reading
It makes me calm
I love to read huge books
It makes me feel like I'm flying
Soothing.

Jack Evans (11)
Steep CE Primary School

Sunshine - Cinquain

Sunshine
How glorious
Blinking at its bright glare
It is matchless in its beauty
Sunshine.

John Mackey (10)
Steep CE Primary School

Autumn - Cinquain

Autumn
It has no leaves
Stepping and crushing down
It's the happiest month to me
Sunny.

Stephen Miller (11)
Steep CE Primary School

Flowers - Cinquain

Flowers
Little pink buds
Roots growing in the soil
Swaying in the nice smiling sun
Lovely.

Ella Williamson (11)
Steep CE Primary School

Butterfly - Haiku

Beauty with colour,
Swooping, soaring like a dart
Dancing on the lawn.

Katriona Pritchard (9)
Steep CE Primary School

Chocolate - Cinquain

Chocolate
Creamy and rich
Melting in the sunshine
A very happy sight to see
Yummy!

Ellie Hitchcock (9)
Steep CE Primary School

Banana Tree Time

I hide in the bushes
Waiting for a sign
The bananas, well, they're all mine
As I approach the tallest tree
I see the bananas staring at me!
Yes, I'm there
Am I moving?
Although yes, it's rather soothing
Ah, that was a hurtful landing.
I wake up with thousands of bananas
On a shelf with toy piranhas!
I've got to get back before it's late,
I'm going to tea with my best mate
I'm coming home on the truck
There's my mate, Muck.
Night-night jungle, see you in the morning
What an adventure, the new day is dawning!

Sophie Topps (10)
Steep CE Primary School

Cackling Witches

Grim Reaper's heart, mouldy potion and blood of phantom,
Vampire's disgusting fangs, elephant's tusks,
Rotting pumpkins, tongue of beaver,
Ghost's howl, flash of lightning, cracking of trees,
Croak of frog and buzz of bees.
Goblin's eyes to cool it down.

Megan Tompkins (8)
Tower Hill Primary School

The Witch's Evil Potion

Ugly horrible witches,
Dead dog's brain,
Shaved cat's tail,
Sheep's furry toe.
Chicken's clucking beak,
Spider's moving legs,
People's beating hearts,
Vampire's dripping fangs.
Shark's filthy tooth,
Bake and boil.

Daniel Beers-Baker (10)
Tower Hill Primary School

Pumpkin Soup

Witch's potions, sweets turn green,
All night it's Hallowe'en.
Spider's blood and worm's google eye,
Wing of bat, eye of frog,
Toe of newt and piece of pumpkin pie,
Skin of snake, lizard nail,
All night it's Hallowe'en!

Klara Cheetham (9)
Tower Hill Primary School

Hallowe'en

A dark, gloomy, haunted house where nobody goes,
The blazing fire dies down to ashes,
A floating shimmering poltergeist comes out of the fog,
Distant screams echoing around the house.

Jordan Greentree (9)
Tower Hill Primary School

Dawn Spell

Witch's wart and giant's weed.

Fraction of moon and tail of rat,
Fireman's toes, wings of a bat.

The laugh of a devil and bubbling cauldron.

A broomstick in pieces would do,
Human urine and ocean blue.

Grim Reaper's slash and skeleton's rattle.

Mix it together with a spoon,
Add the hair of a baboon.

A dangerous, horrifying magic spell.

Alexandra Groves (9)
Tower Hill Primary School

The Flower

The flower grew its lovely way to see the sunny sun
And saw the sky which looked so blue.
But then the rain came but the wind made a brilliant breeze
So it pushed the mean rain away
And the flower was saved . . .
At last it could see the sun!

Megan Stimson (8)
Tower Hill Primary School

Hallowe'en

A spooky, shimmering white ghost,
A dark black werewolf with mighty fangs,
A flickering pumpkin with fearsome eyes,
Petrifying noises scaring all that hear,
Terrifying zombies feasting on human flesh.

George Griffiths (9)
Tower Hill Primary School

Happy Hallowe'en

The shining silver moon,
The werewolf strikes,
The petrifying creatures
Have sharp claws,
Enough to draw blood.
Grim Reaper is watching,
Knows every move,
Scythe slashing magic,
To everything you know.
Hallowe'en's dead rise up,
Meet at the graveyard,
Sitting on tombstones,
Ready to scare.
Ghosts rattling streetlights,
Frightened trick or treaters,
People can't see them,
Happy Hallowe'en.

Matthew Spencer (9)
Tower Hill Primary School

Hallowe'en

Hallowe'en, day of dead,
Evil spirits meeting,
Ghosts are dancing,
Monsters are eating.

Pumpkins' gleaming candlelit eyes,
Looking wherever you go.

Creatures astonished,
Grim Reapers boogying,
Rock zombies rocking,
Bats are flying.

Half a shining moon for me.

George Sidney (10)
Tower Hill Primary School

I Am War!

I am the din of battle.
I am the loss of life, the young fallen soldiers.
I am the reason for the silent sorrow.
I am the wound, forever deep in your heart.
I am the ruby blood scattered across the battlefield.
I am the steep dragon teeth defending my country.
I am the sobbing soldier, all alone on the battlefield.
I am the sound of gunfire, powerful and destructive.
I will never die!

Callum Gribble (10)
Tower Hill Primary School

The Meadow Of Flowers

As I stand in this meadow of stunning flowers,
I can see a magical troop of amazing peachy-pink blooms.
I can hear the busy, buzzing bees collecting nectar
To give to the Queen bee.
As I feel the violet petals on my skin
I can smell the aroma of strawberry jelly.
I feel like the wind wafting through this field of perfect flowers,
Free and peaceful.

Charlie Pearson (11)
Tower Hill Primary School

Shape Poem

The cute and cuddly kitten
pounced through the cat flap.
He rolled past the mat
like a fur ball to get to his food
with a cheeky smile on his face.
Then he bounced away!

Zak De Bruyn (7)
Tower Hill Primary School

I Am War!

I am the mother left behind, devastated; I may not see my son again!
I am the drums, beating until the war begins.
I am a gun, shooting my enemy to save my country.
I am a young soldier, bravely fighting for England.
I am the screaming of the young soldier falling in pain.
I am the bomb flying through the smoky sky.
I am the ruby blood dripping onto the hard ground below.
I am the rusty tank moving to see the battle begin.
I am the grenade travelling towards my evil enemy.
I am a soldier lying dead in the fields where poppies grow.
Always remember the brave soldiers fighting to help us.
They are forever in our hearts.

Chloe Skinner (11)
Tower Hill Primary School

Winter Tree

I am a brawny bear, ferocious and fearless,
guarding my surroundings.
My stern sharp claws root me in the hard, frozen soil.
My slim body is held up by my muscular hind legs.
My fawn fur shines sepia in the setting sun.
As the sun sleeps and the moon awakes,
The wind whistles past as the bear roars.
When the wind stops, the bear is silent!

Connor Griffiths (11)
Tower Hill Primary School

The Kitten

The kitten is cute and cuddly
Its coat is a dull grey colour
It pounces through the cat flap
To get its lunch.

Jordan Sayers (8)
Tower Hill Primary School

I Am A Guard Of Nature

I am a guard of nature,
With my feet firmly in the soily ground.
My straight spine keeps me upright and strong,
Guarding and protecting nature in all weathers.
My skin is dry, rough and weathered,
My bumpy arms sway in the wind,
My fragile fingers snap in the gusty winter.
My head turns to look for danger,
The frosty winter's wind blows away my golden hair.
The cold hard soil is the floor of my house.
The carpet, green, soft and springy,
A sprinkling of 'Shake 'n' Vac' brings the smell of winter.
My furniture is round and spiky,
My orange sky is my rooftop.

Bradley (11)
Tower Hill Primary School

The Meadow

As I stand in this meadow of tropical flowers,
I can see the apple-green flowers growing day by day.
I can smell the scent of roses and honey from the beehive.
I can hear the bees buzzing every day
And the beautiful sounds of paradise.

Rai Hemant Kumar (11)
Tower Hill Primary School

Max

Max is furry and black.
He has a lovely soft coat
And a very waggy tail.
He's fab at tug of war
And nearly pulls me through the door!

James Cook (7)
Tower Hill Primary School

I Am War!

I am the poppies standing straight and proud.
I am the graves for those who guard our country.
I am the body of a fallen soldier, resting proudly,
Knowing I did my best to protect England.
I am the soldiers feeling sad that my fellow comrades have died.
I am the sad but proud mother of the fighting soldiers.
I am the darkness in the soldiers' hearts.
I am the fear that consumes the soldiers as they enter the battlefield.
I am war!
Remember the sacrifice, remember the brave soldiers.

Nadine Drew (11)
Tower Hill Primary School

Tropical Flowers

As I stand in this meadow of tropical flowers,
I can smell scented petals swaying through the cool breeze.
I can see the peaceful colour shimmering as I walk.
I hear the humming of bees hovering above the beautiful blooms.
I can hear the waves lapping on the shore,
And seagulls in the distance.
I feel relaxed as the scent of petals washes over me,
Carried on the wind.

Courtney Bell (11)
Tower Hill Primary School

The Cat

The fluffy cute kitty
Looks like a fluffy ball of wool.
Cheeky, bouncing, happy kitty,
Full of fun,
Watch out!

Nikki Pauline Hayes (8)
Tower Hill Primary School

I Am War

I am a soldier proud to be fighting for my country.
I am a bomb flying through the smoky sky.
I am crimson blood falling to the hard barren ground.
I am a lonely mother watching my son go to war.
I am a graveyard, dark and dull.
I am the dirty, dusty battlefield covered with blood.
I am a ruby poppy worn to remember the fallen men.
Remember us always and never forget.

Kerry Peace (10)
Tower Hill Primary School

Tropical Flowers

As I stand in this meadow of tropical flowers,
I can feel the freedom all around me, in the summer air.
I can hear the sweet sound of buzzing, the sound of nature.
I can see the rainbow colours of the petals
Shimmering in the golden sunlight.
I can smell the sweet scent of the pollen, strong but pretty.

Johnny Whitehead (10)
Tower Hill Primary School

Tropical Flowers

As I stand in this meadow of tropical flowers,
I can see a rainbow blanket, covering the emerald grass.
I can smell the perfume of the sea as the bees collect nectar
And take it back to the queen bee.

Daniel Freke (11)
Tower Hill Primary School

I Am A Soldier

I am a soldier . . .
I am a soldier fighting for my country.
I am a soldier, fierce and proud.
I am a soldier with hope and love in my heart.
I am a lonely soldier, remembering my loved ones at home.
I am a soldier hoping I live or that I die in peace.
I am a soldier, worried but hopeful.

Kitty Roberts (11)
Tower Hill Primary School

The Meadow

As I stand in this meadow of tropical flowers, I can see
exotic petals nodding in the silent breeze, roasting under
the tawny sun, floating in the azure sky.

I can hear the buzzing of insects as they flitter around rainbow flowers,
collecting nectar from crimson and salmon petals.

I can smell a sweet scent floating around my nose.

I feel calm and relaxed, standing on my own in this meadow
of tropical flowers.

Michael Crowhurst (10)
Tower Hill Primary School

Winter Tree

I am a guard of nature with my roots planted firmly
in the solid ground.
My straight spine keeps me upright and strong.
In the cold winter breeze, my rough skin is dry and weathered.
My hair blows wildly and turns from red to golden brown.

Kallum Chivers (10)
Tower Hill Primary School

The Winter Tree

The tree is a fearsome polar bear,
guarding its territory.

It stands strong and proud reaching towards
the ruby-red medallion sunset.

It cries and roars with the wind.

The branches stretch out, long and muscular
and it howls as the cold grasps at its leafless twigs.

With its long gnarled teeth and with its large lumpy roots.
Its long straight back, robust and powerful.

It waits in this lonely spot covered in a soft,
crystal white blanket of snow.

Jordan Powell (10)
Tower Hill Primary School

I Am War!

I am the regiments ready for battle.
I am a sniper ready to shoot.
I am a proud soldier killing my foe, saving my country.
I am the enemy, scared and alone.
I am the grenade flying through the misty sky.
I am the war hero holding my medals, proud and relieved.
I am never forgotten, always remembered.
Poppies, for hope and for life.

Lewis Anderton (11)
Tower Hill Primary School

Winter Tree

I am a strong, fearless soldier, guarding my surroundings.
I stand my ground, tall and proud, hour upon hour till dawn.
My muscular arms stretch out for my weapon across the sky,
My arms stay still.
The glistening sun shines with the ruby medallion sunset,
I gaze upon it with my sapphire eyes.
My strong, steady feet mould into the soil
And my toes crackle across the shivering stones,
But I stay standing, big and bold.
The soft apple grass comforts me,
As I gaze in wonder at why I am here, I think about my family.
My steady and strong tree trunk keeps me balanced
As I stand firm and watch my loved ones!

Tom Spencer (10)
Tower Hill Primary School

Winter Tree

The bare tree is like a strong, fierce troll,
standing in the cold, crispy, crunchy snow.
His hard, rough skin keeps his tall, stiff body warm.
The golden sun shines on his firm back.
At the end of his long skinny arms are his thin, bony hands
and sharp nails.
The sapphire, cloudless sky looks down on the brutal troll
standing rigid and alone.
Other crooked trees stand in the background
wishing they were as strong as this troll.

Selvy Yasotharan (11)
Tower Hill Primary School

Young Writers Information

We hope you have enjoyed reading this book - and that you will continue to enjoy it in the coming years.

If you like reading and writing poetry drop us a line, or give us a call, and we'll send you a free information pack.

Alternatively if you would like to order further copies of this book or any of our other titles, then please give us a call or log onto our website at www.youngwriters.co.uk

**Young Writers Information
Remus House
Coltsfoot Drive
Peterborough
PE2 9JX**

(01733) 890066